# THE LAND OF LOST CONTENT

"A poignant, funny and touching tale, not just about family,
but also about endurance and growth through civil war.
A must for those who want to know about a time
now lost, but not that long ago."

" … a wonderfully evocative description of
family life in the years before the Civil War … "

## BY SURESHINI SANDERS

The Land of Lost Content
Sureshini Sanders

This second edition first published in 2015 by Crescent House.
First published in 2013 by MDPD.

Crescent House
Crescent House, 228 Psalter Lane, Sheffield S11 8UT.

Copyright © Sureshini Sanders 2015.

Photography copyright © Sanders Collection unless otherwise credited.

Sureshini Sanders has asserted her rights under the Copyright, Designs
and Patents Act 1988 to be identified as author of this work.

This book is a work of non-fiction based on the life of Sureshini Sanders.

The author has stated to the publishers that, except in such minor respects not
affecting the substantial accuracy of the work, the contents of the book are true.

A CIP catalogue record for this book is available from the British Library.

ISBN: 978-1-909461-01-7

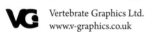 Vertebrate Graphics Ltd.
www.v-graphics.co.uk

Printed and bound in the UK by T. J. International Ltd, Padstow, Cornwall.

For my children Daniel, Rohini,
Samuel, Rajan, Samira and Daniel Jr
and their children and their children

*Into my heart an air that kills*
*From yon far country blows:*
*What are those blue remembered hills,*
*What spires, what farms are those?*
*That is the land of lost content,*
*I see it shining plain,*
*The happy highways where I went*
*And cannot come again.*

A.E. Housman

# ACKNOWLEDGEMENTS

This must be the dullest part of any piece of literature. Who are these people and of what interest are they to the reader? The answer is probably of little interest, but these people are of great value to the author, who really could not have completed the book without them. So, thank you to Dave and Sandra Lennie for all their suggestions on this project and others. My proofreaders Catherine Park, Alex Crawford, Dr Robert Finnie, Dr Gillian Steele, Rohi and Rajan Shah. To my sister Rosh for all your love and support in all my ventures, you were right as always. I feel better now.

Finally, last but not least, to Prem Shah for the beautiful photographs painfully reconstructed. You brought my people back to life.

# FAMILY TREE

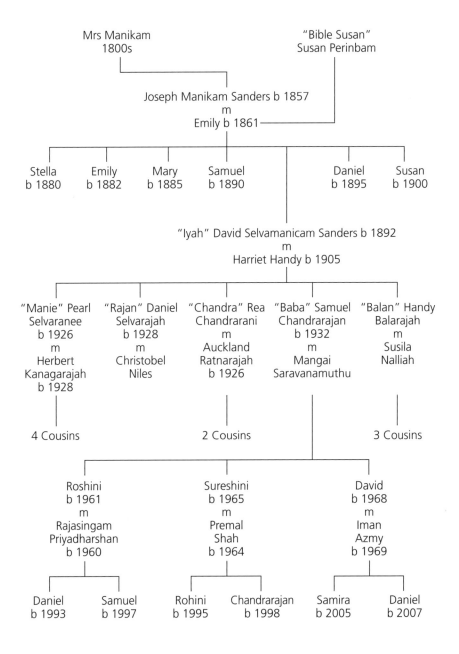

Mrs Manikam
1800s

"Bible Susan"
Susan Perinbam

Joseph Manikam Sanders b 1857
m
Emily b 1861

| Stella b 1880 | Emily b 1882 | Mary b 1885 | Samuel b 1890 | Daniel b 1895 | Susan b 1900 |

"Iyah" David Selvamanicam Sanders b 1892
m
Harriet Handy b 1905

"Manie" Pearl
Selvaranee
b 1926
m
Herbert
Kanagarajah
b 1928

"Rajan" Daniel
Selvarajah
b 1928
m
Christobel
Niles

"Chandra" Rea
Chandrarani
m
Auckland
Ratnarajah
b 1926

"Baba" Samuel
Chandrarajan
b 1932
m
Mangai
Saravanamuthu

"Balan" Handy
Balarajah
m
Susila
Nalliah

4 Cousins

2 Cousins

3 Cousins

Roshini
b 1961
m
Rajasingam
Priyadharshan
b 1960

Sureshini
b 1965
m
Premal
Shah
b 1964

David
b 1968
m
Iman
Azmy
b 1969

| Daniel b 1993 | Samuel b 1997 | Rohini b 1995 | Chandrarajan b 1998 | Samira b 2005 | Daniel b 2007 |

# CONTENTS

# CHAPTER 1

# PARADISE

Have you ever noticed that if something is much loved, it can have many names? For example, mother, mum, mummy, ma or home, house, abode or dwelling place.

We came from a country with many names. Taprobane, Serendib, the Garden of Eden, Resplendent Isle, Pearl of the Indian Ocean, Ceylon, Sri Lanka, Teardrop.

Though once connected by the Palk Straits to India, we had long had our own distinct ways. Telling a Sri Lankan that he is Indian, is like telling a Scotsman that he is French. Britain is an island off France, and Ceylon an island off India; but we are quite different from one another.

When we were children, we thought it the most beautiful place in the world. It was tropical, lush, wet and bursting with life. There were spectacular glistening beaches, the sapphire ocean around us and waving palm trees. In the hill country it was cool, misty and mountainous, and in the north the red, dry earth could still sustain the magnificent palmyra tree; elegant, tall with fan-like palms. The scenery for such a small island was varied and breathtaking. Multicoloured, exotic birds the names of which I could never remember (much to the irritation of my teachers), flew over our heads.

The flora and fauna were like nowhere else and some of it unique to the island, as we had heat and water in abundance. If I shut my eyes and concentrate, I can still smell the overwhelmingly sweet perfume of the temple flower and recall the dazzling colours of the orchids, cannas, bougainvillea and the blood red shoe flower.

When we were little one of our most wicked preoccupations was to steal mangos and cherries from our neighbours. The mangos in the area were renowned and each tree bore fruit with a different flavour. *Karuthu Columban* and *Navapallum* were our favourites.

Before landing, holidaymakers to Ceylon would frequently be subject to a compulsory mini tour. The pilots would show off, rising high and then dipping low above the glittering blue waters and sun-kissed beaches. Passengers would feel as if they could touch the palm trees as they glided past. I was so proud once; surely this was the Garden of Eden and it was mine.

Being an island, the people evolved their own ways. Island peoples can be a little wayward. They do not have the body of the mainland to suffocate their desires and breathe conservatism into their veins. They are allowed to evolve and develop in whichever way they choose. I think it is marvellous to live on an island. Wherever you go and whatever you do, you can quickly make contact with the majestic and mysterious sea.

Even when we migrated to the UK it was the same. It must be claustrophobic to be landlocked. I suppose you could argue that you are then better able to travel and see the world but whether in Ceylon or Britain you can do that and still keep your neighbours at a distance. After all, we have not been set adrift and cut off like the poor souls in Australia. I think if I was surrounded by other countries I would feel threatened and less in control. Pest control, human and animal would become an issue, not to mention land theft.

In Ceylon much controversy arose when neighbours tried to extend their boundaries and re-negotiate land rights. The land was everything and commanded great respect -*Ur*:- Our land. Our God-given inheritance. The land was often inherited from forefathers. If you had it, like us, you were made and if you did not have it, life was not so good.

The island was also blessed with great resources: gems, tea, coffee, spices, paddy fields, coconut and rubber to mention but a few. In later years the rag trade and tourism also helped the economy. Marco Polo was so enamoured that it was he who coined the phrase 'Pearl of the Indian Ocean'. In the fifties and sixties Ceylon was heading the way of Singapore in terms of its GDP and was in direct competition. We all had great hopes for the future. We were the Jewel of the East. We had not had the struggle for independence like India. We were not weary.

You have to leave a place to realise how small it really is. When you have never seen anything else, your world is enormous. In the days when I lived in a small world, I thought myself very important. You have to get out a bit and walk around 'in another man's shoes' to know better. Sri Lanka is a small pearl shaped island: 268 by 139 miles, just north of the equator in the Indian Ocean. It has a population of about 21 million. Only 2 million of her peoples are Tamil and only 10 per cent of this group Christian. As Tamil Christians, that made us a minority in a minority, in a small country.

The days were long and languid and there were only two seasons, rainy season and not rainy season. The weather was never a topic of conversation. I enjoy the four seasons in Scotland so much now and cannot imagine a life without them. As a small island we always had the benefit of sea breezes and the temperature ranged from 24-32 degrees centigrade. I loved the tropical rain which would descend and vanish so unexpectedly. I loved to get soaked and then would gaily march into the house leaving wet footprints, driving my grandfather wild.

The humidity is not so good however; some people found it hard to tolerate but it never bothered me. My main complaint now is that I am always cold. If you speak to people born in the tropics they will often tell you the same, no matter how long they have been away. I am forever waging battle with the cold and lack of sun. On my nostalgic days I go to Butterfly World in Edinburgh, shut my eyes, and am transported back.

We were descendants of the Indus Valley civilisation. In 1600 B.C. Aryans on horseback rode into and destroyed our refined cities. They did not understand our drainage systems or agricultural concepts. Our ancestors moved south and took to the seas, later trading with the Greeks and Romans. Our kingdoms flourished particularly in the Chola, Chera and Pandya eras. People had been living on the island since five thousand BC. Various invaders left their footprint, the Portuguese, Dutch and then the British. The Vedas were the original people on the island and both the Sinhalese and Tamil people came to the island hundreds of years before the birth of Christ. There were Moors on the west coast, descended from Arab traders, Malays and Burghers of Eurasian origin. Many other ethnic groups also lived in Ceylon.

When I was young, just about every day seemed a public holiday as Buddhist, Hindu, Christian and Muslim festivals were all given homage. Ceylon made the most of its foreigners, with much ebbing and flowing of ideas, customs, language, food, dress and marriage. It was a melting pot of forward thinking people, ready to evolve and embrace all that the world had to offer. It seemed as if we had the necessary ingredients to become a very successful little island.

Broadly speaking the Tamils lived in the arid north and the Sinhalese in the fertile south. However, this was not cut and dry; there was a lot of coming and going in those days and it had been so for thousands of years. They said that if you sat on your porch and threw a handful of seeds, they would grow in the south of Ceylon. This made the people here very relaxed and easy going, for life was good. Foreign travellers over the ages always commented that the locals were friendly and hospitable.

The Sinhalese spoke the Sinhala language which when written, is exquisite in appearance, curly and quite distinctive. The Tamils spoke Tamil, an ancient language thought to be 25,000 years old and one of the oldest languages in the world still spoken. We speak it differently from the South Indians however. Whenever I try to speak in Tamil when in India, people say, 'You're Sri Lankan aren't you?'

'How do you know?' I reply in surprise.

'Because you people do not know how to talk properly!'

If you ever observe the Ceylonese, they vary from pale to dark brown. Pale is *vellai* which is desirable and means you are not a labourer, hence rich enough to stay out of the scorching sun. You probably spend endless hours on the veranda, gossiping and eating too many cashew nuts. Dark is undesirable or *Karrupu* this probably means you are a labourer. The world is an extraordinary place, where the pale nations want to be dark, as it implies you can afford foreign travel, and the dark nations want to be pale. All these differences were once celebrated, but later became the source of our troubles.

We had sun everywhere, every day, and used to keep away and hide in our cool stone houses. My daughter sunbathes, which I find hilarious. "You will become *karrupu!*" I shout. She really has no concept of such thoughts and what they may mean to me.

Families engaged in trade or professions. In our family we were ministers, teachers and doctors. Other families were involved in business or agriculture. Everyone generally kept to what they were born to do.

Well off families had live-in servants who could either be treated well, as part of the family, or badly. Servants often served their families for generations. I would like to think that we treated our servants well but looking at this system now, I can see that this was inherently unfair. The positives are that there was a responsibility placed upon wealthier families to look after poorer families over generations. The servant classes were to some extent suppressed and upward mobility was difficult and limited.

Buddhism is practised predominantly by the Sinhalese and is the main religion in Ceylon. It preaches peace, love, tolerance and non-harm to all living things. The island is dotted with ancient dagobas with their distinctive dome-like forms. These are generally in the South but some that were 2000 years old were found in the North as well. Hinduism also preaches peace, love, tolerance and non-harm. Hindu Temples tended to belong to the Tamils in the North. They were completely different; colourful, peaked structures, with amazing statues carved on to them. In contrast, the Christian churches were rather humble. As a child, I loved all religions because they meant school holidays, festivals and food.

In previous centuries when our kingdom flourished you could see this acceptance and understanding as Buddhist and Hindu icons stood side by side in the ancient city of Polonnaruwa, and Hindu gods stood guard over moonstones. This was an eleventh century city but Anuradhapura, at fourth century BC was older still.

We were more civilised then and our country, with many different kingdoms and kings, flourished. The ruins of palaces can still be seen, some of which were several stories high. There was even a Tamil king on a Sinhala throne at one point and intermarriage commonly occurred to secure lands and kingdoms.

In these early times frescos depicted exotic voluptuous female figures. I always found them strange, as they looked like no one I knew. Had we so changed through the centuries?

Traditionally men wore cotton sarongs to keep themselves cool but nowadays these traditional outfits tend to be for festivals and special occasions. The women wear saris but the Sinhalese ladies have a distinct way of dressing it, with a fan to one side. The fabrics are vast in range and quality but I do think a ban should be imposed on plump elderly ladies wearing them. The sari is very elegant but as it takes me half an hour to put on properly, intricate complex folds which never come right, I do not bother. The other drawback is that it is not easy to move around in and if you, like me, are accident prone and step on it, you can suddenly find yourself compromised as six yards of silk cascade to the floor.

My paternal family lived in Nallur in the north and were surrounded by their own kind. This inheritance was to be both the making and the breaking of our small close knit community. For many years it had been that way for my family. We grew up in a secure environment and everyone knew everyone through marriage, work, school or church. If you misbehaved, aunty was sure to tell your mother or any other relative she could get hold of.

Our house was always full of chatter and heaving with visitors and relatives. Most educated people spoke in English so that all parties could be understood. My parents chose to live in the south of the island, in Colombo, where I was born. My first language was Sinhala, then English and lastly Tamil. Language only lives if it is spoken and now I speak only English fluently, which is a source of regret and shows what little progress I have made linguistically in my life.

My mother seemed to spend vast quantities of time in our cooled store rooms or larder, instructing servants on the preparation of various foods. Meals were always a big affair with a large breakfast, morning coffee, lunch, tea and a modest dinner to organise daily. Everything was freshly prepared and 'old food' was frowned upon. We ate voracious quantities but were still slim because we were always out and about and sweated it off!

As well as enjoying all my meals I also loved the rolls and patties that my grandmother used to make. We have many unusual foods in Ceylon, but it took me thirty years and a trip to Portugal to realise that we had adapted some of these from our invaders. It is unlikely that they stole these ideas from us and that these were then adopted by the whole Portuguese nation. Even then I used to eat until I felt sick, and my grandmother used to say, 'Child, you must stop yourself before you are totally full or your belly will ache.'

You rarely had a moment to yourself unless you were ill or being eccentric. I accepted that then and found it reassuring but as I get older I think this may have started to bother me. Our visitors came from the many ethnicities within the island, as my parents had an eclectic mix of friends. Some of our visitors would stay for dinner uninvited. If anyone did this now, I would be quite irritated but catering is easy with servants. If you feel so inclined, you too could reciprocate and intrude upon your neighbours and family in similar fashion. It was a tradition.

Mostly we spent our days with an early rise, going to school or work, afternoon nap, then back again. Eating took forever and lunch was the most important meal of the day. A lot of time was spent on the veranda with family and friends, as were the holidays. Uncles and aunts would go abroad to obtain post graduate degrees in the UK or Singapore but they always came home in the end. If you were poor you just stayed where you were and hoped that God would be kinder in the next life.

In those days, the biggest battles were fought on the cricket pitch. This was a national obsession and school boys from the leading island schools of Royal and Thomian would have long, heated debates about who was best and why. I still smile recalling two of my male cousins, who were at different schools, and though on very good terms generally, when it came to this issue nearly came to blows.

Darkness descends quickly in the tropics; before you know it the sun has crashed, exhausted, and embraced the horizon. The day is done. Wherever we ventured we knew most people in our area, so we never worried about our safety. Eventually someone would send word that the cricket games were to be wound up and we had to go home.

There was no TV at night but we could read or play *carroum* or cards. If we were very lucky one of my cousins, who was a fantastic cartoonist, would turn up. She was a crack animator and provided free entertainment for all. There were also cousins who played the piano or sang or danced or told stories. In fact there was a cousin for just about everything.

Sundays meant church, lunch and quiet time, except for more visitors. If you were really good there may have also been a trip to an ice cream parlour or the latest movie *imported*. Most people could afford some treats as we were a country without the extremes of wealth and poverty in the fifties and sixties.

Nothing moved fast. It was a pattern of life that had been the same for generations. We lived and studied and worked mostly in the same areas and when we died we were all buried together at St James' in Nallur, Jaffna. When we went to church, I used to imagine that at night all my dead relatives would rise up and start chattering over each other, as they did in life. I thought to myself, 'I'll be joining you one day, but not today.'

I visited the graveyard in 2005 – it looked dreadful, ancient and musty. An empty place where the dead lay uncared for, by a people long gone.

For we had no idea, or maybe we did and ignored it, that this Utopia would all come suddenly to an abrupt halt. Everything would change forever and we would be flung all over the globe, never to return. The idyllic lives we had enjoyed were to be no more. Our resplendent island in the sun, our pearl of the Indian Ocean, was about to be transformed to a teardrop of sorrow.

CHAPTER 2

# A DIFFICULT LADY

What drives a person to give up everything they know because of their calling or religion? Does it show a selfish, arrogant individual with little regard for the feelings of others, or maybe a free spirit who is inspired and has no fear?

One action can change the entire course of a family's destiny. Women are powerful creatures. For all the saris and jewels and gentle curves, many of the Sanders women knew exactly what they wanted. Their charge was the most important task of all; the care of their children and family.

My great-great-grandmother was born in the early 1800s, in Jaffna, the largest region in the north. Dates are vague before this because Hindus do not regard birthdays as important, in the way that Christians do. I suppose if you are planning to be reborn several times, it is of little significance in the grand scheme of things.

In contrast, Christians were diligent at documenting records and keeping paperwork. Hindus relied more on oral history. The bombing of the Jaffna library resulted in the destruction of all our ancient documents and the disbanding of our people so I will never be able to go back further than my great-great-grandmothers. This was a moment of genius, which ethnically cleansed us of our history. All I know is that we were Hindu and well off.

We were probably involved in business ventures and our name was Manikam. My great great-grandmothers came from the districts of Uduvil and Tellipallai.

I do not even know the first name of my Sanders great-great-grandmother but she became Mrs Manikam and had a son. She was a free thinker and at that time an American missionary by the name of Rev. Sanders was preaching in the north of the island. She fell under the spell of a loving, forgiving God, who treated all men as equals. Her husband was understandably unhappy about this, for there was no need for her to stand shoulder to shoulder with low-caste people and accept this fantasy. She in her wisdom kept attending Rev. Sanders' sermons, as did one of her friends.

In exasperation poor Mr Manikam threatened to throw her out but she was 'not for turning'. She not only left with her son, but changed her name to Sanders, a Christian surname. Her friend did much the same and thus it was that there came to be two Sanders families in Ceylon, as it is to this day. They are not related in any way, save by the faith of these ladies. The other Sanders family went into the police force in the main and were renowned sportsmen. I remember once seeing a picture in a magazine of one of them; a very dapper young man. I was disappointed to find that we were not related. We were a much more sedate crowd involved in the church, teaching and medicine.

If you ever see an Asian with a name that does not match his appearance, especially if it is a biblical name like Joseph, Mary or David, the odds are that they are Christian, not that this has been a recent name change with migration.

In one action my great-great-grandmother deprived her child of a comfortable existence and chose instead a calling to God, a life of the spirit and financial instability. Did she ever have regrets? Who knows?

She named her son Joseph Manikam Sanders.

I still cannot understand why her husband did not put up more of a fight, or at least insist that his son remain in his care. Perhaps he thought it was easier to write them both off as a mistake and start again. In another account of this tale Mrs Manikam is widowed and then takes her leave upon her husband's death. Even so, I am amazed that no one tried to stop her.

Her actions changed our fate. From then on we were to be Christian and out of sync with the majority of the island who were either Buddhist or Hindu. Would we still be there today if not for her? Would we have been gone altogether?

Two types of people converted to Christianity: there were those who saw greater opportunity, especially because a lot of the mission schools offered better education and prospects of employment irrespective of caste, and those who truly believed. The British Empire promoted the Christian faith.

Mrs Manikam and her son lived and worked in the American Mission. She made great friends with a lady called Susan Perinbam, nicknamed 'Bible Susan'. This lady was quite a convincing preacher and went around the district assisting the minister and converting people. Mrs Manikam seems to have had a quieter life once in the Mission. Susan had a daughter called Emily who became Joseph's dearest playground companion. To the mothers' delight, as they came into adult life, they decided to marry and Joseph became a minister having completed a theology course at Jaffna College.

Emily was the ideal minister's wife. She had spent some time in the Christian Girls' Boarding school at Udupiddy and so this, and her mother's teachings, imbibed a yearning for evangelism. She later became headmistress of the Station Girls' School and assisted her husband ably in church work.

They said of Joseph that although he was a good preacher, many people were attracted to the faith because of his wife's singing. At moonlight meetings her alluring voice would help gather the crowds.

Emily facilitated in educating the local girls and encouraged them to useful employment. She also started a sewing circle, which was like a modern day women's guild. Here women gathered and chatted and supported each other. They became empowered together.

The Mission compounds were the centre of all village activity and often the pastors were the only people who were English speaking and hence were influential in mediating between the local population and the British government.

Joseph also helped to translate local and foreign news and government circulars for publication in the Tamil Biweekly.

His greatest achievement, however, was to secure the funding for the building of the Atchuvely Church. He chose a site where the remains of a four hundred year old Portuguese church once stood in Atchuvely, a town in north Jaffna. This brought on the wrath of prominent Catholic and Hindu members of the district but he was not to be deterred.

His wife worked her charm on the ladies of the community too and eventually their dreams were realised; they even managed to get the opposition to attend church on a few occasions and converted some of their children! The church stands to this day and in 1887 Joseph became its pastor. It is not large but quaint and within its walls an orphanage exists 'to help the helpless'. It is in this church that several generations of Sanders children were christened for nearly one hundred years, until 1970.

Joseph and Emily had a fruitful marriage and seven children over twenty years, three sons and four daughters. My grandfather David was their second son, and schooled in Jaffna College. He then travelled to Calcutta where he became an arts graduate from Calcutta University in 1919, as it was a centre of excellence in South East Asia. Subsequently he trained in The University College, Colombo too.

Jaffna College was an American Mission School and one of the leading institutions in the north of Ceylon. The three Sanders brothers were fiercely loyal to their alma mater and all taught there. Between them, the Sanders served the school for over one hundred years. Samuel, the eldest became the bursar; my grandfather, vice-principal and Daniel, the first scout and games master of the college.

Joseph died when nearly sixty, which was not a bad innings, as globally the average age for demise in the early 1900s was mid-forties.

His wife survived for nearly two decades after him. The blight of her latter life was that their brightest and most handsome youngest son, Daniel, died ten years before her.

He had taken a group of boys on a scouting trip and contracted typhoid. He was in his twenties and had never married. Several children over the generations have been named after him, and in truly unimaginative style I currently have two nephews both called Daniel. So, the original has lived on in a way he may not have imagined. My grandfather adored his youngest brother and even in old age would become silent and pensive if asked about him.

Of Joseph's and Emily's four daughters, one married another Jaffna College master. One had a husband who sounds as if he had mental health issues and wrote laborious letters to Churchill and another wed my grandmother's older brother. The favourite of all however, became a Mrs Richards. Her husband died when she was young but rather than mourn the rest of her life, she got on with a show of great independence and became a source of love and support to all around her.

Her home was a haven for her nieces and nephews and she mothered and spoilt them all in turn. She inherited her parents' house in Atchuvely and when she died gifted it to one of her nephews. For some reason a number of

Sanders wives have often ended up alone or bereaved early, even in this generation. They have generally shown great stoicism and proven themselves very resilient. Unlike on my mother's side, no one ever remarried.

Emily remained in Atchuvaly till her death in 1930. During this period she continued to lead the mothers meeting regularly every Tuesday and teach in Sunday school.

The role of Ceylonese women has evolved a lot in the last three decades. From mothers, wives, daughters and sisters we have been transformed into main bread winners and 'freedom fighters' with the onslaught of civil war.

Women in Ceylon were thought to be quite liberated, even hundreds of years before. Ancient travellers were horrified that our women sat on the porch with their men folk and were included in discussions on all topics of conversation. They were also disgusted to see that these 'brazen' ladies of all ages exposed their arms and midriffs. (How times have changed and these garments are now thought of as demure, if not submissive.)

The task of mothering was regarded as being the most important and then the role of wife, daughter or sister. Interestingly it is the women who inherit the land in Ceylon, which on reflection is probably a bad idea, as then it was lost to the family. The British system of giving the land to the oldest son, though harsh, keeps it in the family, so to speak. Our land was divided, so once a father split this between his daughters, it and all its assets, were quickly disbanded. Depending on the number of daughters, this could happen in one generation.

It was assumed in those times that a woman did not work, and so the gifts of land and jewellery upon marriage afforded ladies leverage and position. Men worked and did not marry until later, once they had established an income. This all seems good and fair but the system became corrupt as families insisted on a 'dowry' and even working girls were expected to provide this. Though the caste system operated, it was more loosely binding than in India. Nevertheless people tended to marry within their caste. The highest caste were the priests or Brahmins. We had no untouchables. Foreigners would be thought of as no caste, rather than low caste, which I am sure, was a great consolation to them!

The literacy rate in Ceylon was one of the highest in Asia and women bene-fitted from this. It was only in the seventies however that it became common place for women to work. In my mother's generation being a mother, caring for your relatives and running a good home was what was expected.

Food was all important; providing for all who came your way and out-shining each other with culinary prowess. I think the pendulum has swung too much the other way now, as women across the world attempt to multi-task and do all of this, as well as hold down a full time job.

One of my heroes, Jamie Oliver, has exposed poor school meals. I too believe a good diet is one of life's essentials and one of our greatest responsibilities as women is to feed our children. The epidemic of obesity and inertia is partly due to our absence from the home. Men have rarely embraced this role in the past and I remain to be convinced that many of them will desire it in the future. Perhaps we need to accept this and find a better way forward.

I am no saint in this matter. In spite of knowing better, I too have micro-waved meals, shoved children in front of a box and taken a plethora of parenting short cuts, and always for a good reason.

I think life then was easier for all concerned in some ways, as roles in the past were so clearly defined. It could be argued that we did not have much choice, but too much choice leads to chaos. Many of these systems have remained unchallenged for centuries partially because they work.

Mothers taught their daughters how to dress and cook and behave. Fathers instructed their sons. Now we leave it to the soaps and reality television. In Ceylon the civil war led to a breakdown of many of the old ways.

Daughters rather than sons were also expected to care for their parents. In India it is the reverse and so I said to my children, 'How lucky I am, since you are half and half. You will both be fighting to care for me.' They replied that as they live in Scotland, they would be sure to check me into a nice nursing home!

This caring role on top of everything else is very difficult for women, as employers globally want reliable service and domestic issues are your problem, not theirs.

Women then and to some extent now, rarely rose to the top of their professions. There was clearly discrimination afoot but many women simply did not want to, as they saw their role at work as secondary to their role at home.

And yet Ceylon elected the first female prime minister in the world, so that must say something. The Tiger movement also 'boasted' the first unit of female freedom fighters in the world. Luxurious black locks were cut and saris and bangles were swapped for khaki and cyanide capsules. It is so sad to think that these lovely young things felt that this was the only way forward.

They lost their youth, and many their lives for the cause.

The women and men of Sri Lanka have suffered much hardship and, a bit like British women after the Second World War, it is difficult to go back to the way things used to be.

I wonder what Mrs Manikam would think, if she could see her offspring now. Once troubles broke out it was easier for us as Christians and English speakers to migrate to places like Britain, Australia and America. We have all integrated quickly into these countries and moved on with our lives.

If we had remained Hindu, would we still be there today, struggling away, a subjugate people in a war-torn land?

You could argue that we have become 'coconuts'. That is 'brown on the outside and white on the inside'. Once you have abandoned your land, language, dress and much of your diet, what exactly makes you Ceylonese?

Of Mrs Manikam's female descendants there are doctors, accountants and engineers. Some have married and some have not, some have children and some have not. There is quite a range to choose from and much to be proud of but have we really done well, as we have abandoned many of our traditional values?

The unpaid task of being a mother or carer is so undervalued and yet in many ways is the most unselfish and loving of labours. As we have entered 'a modern world', we seem to have been abandoned, to do it all. Many of our female ancestors were supported and cherished. Today we are less looked after and frequently over stretched.

When my mother had her children she was pampered and protected for the first six weeks postpartum. There was enormous support given by relatives. Grandmothers would arrive and cooks would be instructed to concoct protein rich meals to build up the new mother. The baby was often removed to give her peace and rest, so my mother rapidly became plump and inert.

Many mothers now are expected to get on with it and return to work post haste. No surprise therefore that a number get depressed, sleep deprived and miserable.

I wonder how my ancestor managed by herself. The church was all embracing and would have looked after her I am sure and she gave back, in a sense, with her son who served the church. No doubt women then suffered in silence sometimes and certainly had less opportunity than we do but everything comes at a cost.

The civil war has held women back in Sri Lanka. Many have lost their lives and some their children or men folk. Perhaps in time they will find their place again.

My daughter tells me often 'Whatever happens mum, I really don't want to be like you.' So good to inspire the young. She does not want to be like grandma either and stay at home. Maybe the next generation will get it right and find a middle path. We can only live in hope.

# CHAPTER 3

# SANDERS MASTER

My grandfather was born on the 27th of November 1892. He was the fifth child and second son of Joseph and Emily. They called him David Selvamankian Sanders.

He was headstrong, even as a child and much pampered by his elder sisters. Dutiful and diligent he studied in Jaffna College from the age of thirteen and served the school until the end of his working life.

He was sinewy and, for a Ceylonese in those days, tall at 5' 10". The school, keen to promote and keep him, funded his training at Calcutta University.

In those days people feared foreign travel. His parents worried that he would enjoy a one way trip, but it proved not to be so. He returned to teach, majoring in mathematics, ethics, English and Latin. He remained loyal to Jaffna College for all of his life, even in times of strife and when others may have jumped ship. He felt the college had been responsible for his education and he would give back all he could.

Today we all move around and such loyalties are rare. We talk of portfolio careers and opportunities but the concept of lifelong service has long gone. Likewise, institutions are less loyal to employees, hiring and firing without a care.

Grandfather was a somewhat stern but fair individual and much respected by his pupils. He, like my father could be at once sarcastic and hilarious. A good debate was an aperitif to him and he was the Patron of the Brotherhood – Senior Literary Society.

He also became warden of the Inner Hostel of Jaffna College, and president of the Y.M.C.A. He felt great responsibility for his charges and if someone had a problem and could argue their case, he would find a solution to their difficulties.

On one occasion there was a demonstration about the poor quality of food on campus. As war time rations caused a challenge to the cooks, an impasse was forming between them and the students. The students then started to get quite rowdy and there was a lot of shouting and banging of pots and pans. My grandfather was called to deal with this rabble and made his inquiries about the nature of the complaint. Having decided that they were justified, he instructed the serving of mutton, a great treat at the time, and received a standing ovation. From then on he took a personal interest in the diet of his students and bore no grudges against the ring leaders, even though he always knew who they were!

He was often seen walking along the corridors of the school in measured steps in full suit of darker shades. On entering the class he would write down the maths problems for the day. The pupils would laboriously attempt to work these out and he would rattle out a solution with no reference to books or notes. I think I may have struggled in his classes.

When he taught at Jaffna College, we heard that the pupils used to sing:

> *D.S. Sanders master, enna cholar am*
> *Quaduratic equation chai a cholar am*
> *Copy pani condu carta a naught a potar am*

To paraphrase, this means when he asked you to do your equations, if you cheated, he smiled quietly because he somehow always knew and simply gave you nothing for your efforts.

This chant also leads me to explain something else about Ceylon. Many were trilingual and so the spoken word seamlessly included Sinhala, Tamil and English. For example *'Hello darling be a kunchu* ('dear' in Tamil) *and bring me vathura'* ('water' in Sinhala).

He also enjoyed teaching ethics, with the spiritual background of his forefathers. I sometimes wonder why he did not become a minister himself.

In those days masters were much respected and virtually lived, worked and socialised within the grounds of the school. One of his pupils said of him that he was 'always correctly attired, full of poise, dignity and uprightness, ever punctual and devoted to duty. He wielded great influence over his students and won their respect and esteem.'

The time eventually came when a new principal was to be elected in Jaffna College. My grandfather was never a demonstrative man and did not believe in pushing himself forward or flashy campaigns. Here he made a critical error, as this left some wondering if he actually wanted the job. He felt that he had given his life to the college and that his credentials were self-explanatory. But he was described by colleagues as 'shunning ambition'.

One of his former pupils, a Mr Selliah, was not quite so shy however and canvassed long and hard. Needless to say he then went on to become the first national principal of Jaffna College. This must have broken my grandfather's heart but he said nothing and continued his service and assisted Selliah in all matters without bitterness. He was offered posts as principal in other schools but such was his loyalty that he stuck as vice-principal until the end. Had it been me, I would have jumped ship in humiliation.

You cannot put a good man down, however, and right at the end of his working life, he was given the prestigious post of inspector of American Mission Schools.

Masters then, as now, were not very well paid but their reward was in the pupils they taught and inspired. Many of my grandfather's pupils remember him even today and say that he helped forge their careers and aspirations. He had a note of them all in his head and was keenly aware of their progress.

At a party in London recently an old man asked my brother if he was a relative of 'the famous D.S. Sanders'. He was about to reply that he was D.S. Sanders until it dawned on him that the gentleman was referring to our grandfather. No mention of dad or the rest of us less memorable individuals.

There is still a boarding house in Jaffna College named Sanders House and memorial prizes in his name. One of these was funded this year, by the cumulative efforts of all his grandchildren abroad. I think he would be so happy to think that children from less privileged backgrounds are given opportunity and education in his name. He did not care what religion or caste or sex these children were and felt that a good education was an essential to which all children should be entitled.

My father and sister sometimes complained that my grandfather was hard on them but I never found him so. I think with his teaching background he was very instinctive about his people management and was gentle with the vulnerable and harsher on more challenging individuals.

When my parents had to come to Britain to sit exams, we children were to be boarded but my brother at two, was too young. My grandfather was seventy eight years old then and my father, with some trepidation, asked if he would take care of my brother. His curt response was that he would have 'them all or none of them'. He felt we would be traumatised enough without having to be split up as well.

Thus it was that he inherited three children under ten and we went to live with him and my grandmother at Guru Vasa. Everyone called my grandfather 'Iyah' which meant 'Sir'.

Iyah and Appammah (father's mother) lived in Guru Vasa, Nallur South, in Jaffna, north of Ceylon. The land was owned by an ancestor called Guru Nagar. Guru means 'learned one or spiritual leader' and Vasa means house.

By the time we arrived, Iyah had softened with age and was living his retired life enjoying gardening and agriculture. The grounds around Guru Vasa were more than adequate to keep him fit and fully occupied.

He almost became a small time agriculturalist growing his own produce and keeping goats and chickens. There were mango, pawpaw, lime and lemon trees, as well as drumstick and curry leaf trees. He enjoyed these "farming" pursuits and found them to be therapeutic after such a demanding professional life.

When his goat Nita had babies, he let us keep them like pets and consequently they were very affectionate and sweet. Eventually the land could not sustain them all and they had to go. There were tears from all the children and Iyah ensured that they were sold for milk, rather than meat, where possible.

I was like his 'little lamb' and used to follow in his wake. With the curiosity of an abandoned and often inquisitive child, I tagged along with him relentlessly and watched his every move.

There was a regular rhythm to his day and movements. However hard you tried he was always up before everyone else. I never saw him get out of bed in the morning. By the time I emerged from slumber he was usually in the darkest corner of the lounge. A small light would be on and he would be reading his Bible and thinking his thoughts for the day. You disturbed him at your peril. This was followed by listening to the BBC World Service on the radio.

Later he would join us for breakfast, which was a full blown affair. Revolting goats milk, *string hoppers* (a bit like tangled up spaghetti), vegetables and usually fish. Tea was also in vast supply but you were not allowed to drink much until after eating, in case you did not eat enough.

He would chew through this feast with precision and I would watch the veins on his head. I found it very funny how they wriggled around like worms on his temples as he ate. It's never good to laugh too loudly, as I too have them now.

He would then take his leave and attend to his chores around the grounds. There were animals to be fed and milked, eggs to be collected and produce to harvest.

He walked everywhere and kept very fit. He was quite odd about it and would sometimes order a car to take us to church but walk himself. There was no way my grandmother was walking to functions like weddings, funerals and college events. When he was working, he owned a majestic Austin with a chauffeur but he decided upon retirement that this was extravagant and unnecessary.

There were frequent trips to town and we ate fresh food only and there was no concept of freezing or keeping old food. Waste was minimal and the animals consumed what we did not.

I was always losing or breaking things and relied on his trips to town to make good what I had damaged or lost. I would wait until he left the house and went down to the corner of the street. There was a crucial point when he could still hear me shouting but had gone too far to be bothered to return and was too dignified to shout back at me.

'Iyah I have lost my pen!' I would holler. He would swing round and I would get the look and then he would be off. By the time he got home, he forgot to be angry and I got yet another pen.

He was a man who never missed a meal and kept almost exactly to time. He would come home for lunch and then be off again to visit a friend or relative. I used to go with him sometimes. My sister felt too old to do this and my brother was too young; he could not keep still and had little interest.

Many people sought his council and I would try to sit patiently and listen to the chat. Sooner or later I would get fed up with the intellectual ramblings and ruminations of old men. At this point I would start tugging on his trousers and eventually he would give in and we would depart. If I got lucky I would get a treat at the store or 'kaddai' across the street.

Later in the day we would sit on the veranda and eat monkey nuts, read or if I was really good play 'what's the time Mr Wolf?' He never caught me when it was 'Time to eat you up', for although a little chubby, I could move quite fast.

On one occasion when we were together he jumped out of his chair with lightning speed and headed for me with his slipper. He looked like a man possessed and I thought he had gone mad, until I realised that a scorpion was making its way towards us. He had swatted it dead in one shot. He was my hero from then on.

When the monsoon rains came in a deluge, we would construct paper boats and race them. I loved to stand in the rain, as did my sister, much to my grandparents' dismay.

I was constantly in trouble at school for one thing or another but he never lost his patience with me. In my time in Jaffna I never grew an inch or made much academic progress, in spite of all of my grandparents' efforts. He wrote to my father that 'Roshini understands what is happening and David is too small but *Chuttu* is pining for you'. He understood my problems more than anyone else.

In the evening some of my grandmother's friends would come. They would sit and cackle and gossip staying beyond their welcome. Sooner or later Iyah's dinner would be delayed and he lost no time in being rude to them. My grandmother would be furious with him, and my sister and I loved watching the not-so-polite exchanges that then ensued.

Sometimes he would play the piano and we found this very odd, as he was never formally taught but could play some quite complex pieces with finesse and a great understanding of the tune. When, like me, you plod from grade to grade, dutifully practise and *still* manage to produce only half-baked sounds, this is not encouraging.

He used to spend a lot of time thinking quietly, or he would go to his study and write. This was the one place I was forbidden to enter and so the one place I wanted to be. Once, I was really enjoying myself ferreting about his office, when I heard his shuffled steps coming my way. I started to panic, as there was only one way in and out of the room. I had a moment of genius however and hid under his desk. He had long skinny legs, so with careful positioning it was possible to navigate away from them and bide my time. It was not a comfortable hour or a fun way to spend the day, so I did not return for some time.

He spent hours in his study, always writing something and keeping a regular journal for years. He was an eloquent writer, in the way of a Victorian. What I would give to see those journals. What did he write about?

The study also had some old photographs, pictures of long gone relatives in ballooning dresses and austere frock coats. They all looked a bit grumpy to me. People in modern photographs always look much more relaxed and happier. Presumably having your picture taken then was a serious affair, not to be taken lightly. Either that or I possess relatives who were all clearly in need of Prozac.

In the evenings we would all sit together. In this pre-television era, we had to keep each other entertained, usually by reading or playing games. Best of all there would be a power cut and Iyah would shout and the servants scuttle for candles. It was a big old house and took on a very creepy atmosphere in the dark. There were high ceilings with wooden beams and lizards would scurry up the white walls and look like prehistoric monsters coming to get you.

My sister and I shared a bedroom and my grandparents were in another bedroom past the lounge, at the other end of the house. This did not stop us hearing Grandfather's snores which rattled the walls. He would stop and start, stop and start. On one occasion he stopped so long, that we gathered around his bed because we thought he had died. He suddenly jumped up with a sixth sense that he was being watched and we all screamed, terrified.

Another favourite place for a nap was his planter's chair. This was situated with precision on the veranda from whence he had a great view of all that we were up to. Even when you were sure he was fast asleep and you finally got up to some mischief, he would bellow at you and stop you in your tracks. Did he have X-ray eyes as well?

One of my cousins used to love standing at the gate, which was behind him, and chat to passing people. This drove him crazy as he thought it idle gossip-ing and he could always tell when she was doing it, even though she was some distance away, not visible and speaking quietly.

Iyah wanted all of his sons and daughters to stay in Ceylon and was bitterly disappointed when his eldest son Daniel left the island.

My uncle Daniel had gone to Colombo University and studied sociology. It was his life's passion but he was ahead of his time. There was no place for this or understanding of the subject in Ceylon in the fifties. People looked after their own, what need for social work? He migrated to America and talked and published worldwide on the subject. In the end my uncle became a professor of sociology and then dean of the University of Illinois. My grandfather was very proud of his son, but he missed him dearly.

When my uncle left, my grandfather told him that he would never find peace, as once you step on the plane you will look for Ceylon everywhere, and when you come home you will miss what you had abroad.

One by one his children left, so he resorted to communication by mail and composed letters which were astute and informative, written in black ink and the Queen's English. The recipients, usually children or grandchildren, used to collect them. When my aunt went to Australia, she let my sister who was visiting see her collection. One of them read as follows:

*My dearest Eldest child Manie,*
*I understand that you are contemplating leaving the shores of our island. Have you truly considered what impact this will have on you and your growing family? Think carefully before you take this monumental step …*

He witnessed what he thought was his family disbanding unnecessarily. He did not like it but I think he secretly thought it all a transient folly. They would be back in time and realise what they had given up. He would simply bide his time and wait.

Throughout his life there had been the odd riot and unrest. Independence came easily to us but pockets of dissent were arising. Up country Sinhalese thought they were better than low country Sinhalese. Ceylon Tamils thought they were better than Indian Tamils and at one point there was even a communist party.

When we were staying with him in 1972, we went one evening to an outdoor passion play. We were all very excited about this, as my grandparents had a conservative lifestyle and were particularly cautious with us, as we were not their children. In short, we did not get out much. Suddenly a bomb went off whilst we were at the play and people were running in all directions. In typical Ceylonese style we took this in our stride and naively thought it would all get better another day.

This was an aperitif to what was to come. It was at this time that Ceylon was renamed Sri Lanka and the old Ceylonese ways, tolerant, all encompassing, gave way to Sri Lankan patriotism. I am glad my grandfather died in 1980 and did not see what happened next.

I got a lot from my grandfather. I soaked him up like a sponge. Amazing how you can live many years, travel to many places and meet a variety of people, but those days, weeks and months spent with him were, and are, a footprint upon my soul.

I liked the way he took his time. I liked his silence and his sarcastic observations, especially because they were never directed at me. He was so clear about right and wrong and no believer in grey areas. I liked to watch him navigate the day, read his Bible, write his correspondence, take his walks and lovingly tend his property.

He exemplified the best of East and West in many ways. He was a learned man of faith and principles and prepared his students and children well for the outside world. He thought that the British had a lot to offer with their attitude to time keeping and order but was also proud of his Ceylonese roots and culture.

Though deeply Christian, he had respect for all people. He never ate beef and would light candles in homage of the cow, like the Hindus. One day my father had been disrespectful to the *dobbie* (washer of clothes), who was low caste, and got a swift slap for his trouble.

It could be argued that my grandfather's approach to life was too simple, too black and white. I too am often accused of this and I think people of greater intelligence can see the world from another's perspective and different angles. There was something simple about my Iyah but this made for an easier life. He did not clutter his head with foolish thoughts and wants. He enjoyed all he had and was grateful for it.

He had a bright, keen mind until the end. When finally he had a stroke he was nearly ninety. My grandmother was trying valiantly to look after him at home and in his usual selfless way, he told her it was too much for her. He was then transferred to a private hospital and was clearly dying.

A physiotherapist was advised to try to get him going. The therapist obviously had no knowledge of his patient, as if my grandfather could have moved, he would have moved. Iyah, frustrated at the man's lack of insight, eventually said to him, 'Young man, do you think you are preparing me for the Olympics?'

25

When he died he was buried at his request at St James Church in Nallur with my grandmother's people. Four generations of her family, including her father, were laid to rest there, in a large mausoleum. He thought she would like this and that he would be waiting for her with them. His gravestone is engraved with a simple message to us all that depicted his way of life: 'In faith is the victory.' His descendants would all agree that this was his legacy to us – faith, and a code of behaviour second to none.

A country in turmoil is not a place you can easily visit and wars rob people. You are told that he is dead but you cannot see him. You cannot attend the funeral, you cannot kiss his face. You cannot say goodbye. There is no coffin, no grave and no mourners come. You are in a cold country, half a world away. So, in your head, he is alive. You see his chiselled face in the half light of the study. His deep voice informs you that he is headed down the Navallar Road, to town on some errand. He is striding away. You wait a minute hoping he has gone far enough, a fine judgement call. If you get it wrong this time you will be in big trouble; still you risk it and shout,

'Iyah I've lost my pen again.'

# CHAPTER 4

# WELCOME TO THE HANDY FAMILY

I have often been accused of looking back on our old life with 'rose tinted spectacles' but even I could not claim that my grandmother Harriet was beautiful in appearance. What she possessed was a beautiful mind. It shone with its brilliance and when you see old photographs of her, you can see it in her eyes. She was like many of her family, energetic and effervescent.

Her father was Rev. C.C. Handy, a well-known minister in Nallur and the first 'native' principal of St John's College. She clearly got her brain from him, but sadly was not to ever know him as anything but some sort of mythical figure, as he passed away when she was but three years old.

One hundred years later, I came to find some documentation on how this happened and realised that he had diabetes. This brought tears to my eyes as in today's world his death would have been so easily preventable. It frustrated me that I could not go back in time and say, 'Inject yourself with this twice a day and you'll be fine.'

His young widow had five children to bring up aged from three to fourteen years of age. The only silver-lining in this very dark cloud over her life was her father Rev. John Backus. Fortunately my great-great-grandfather was wealthy and provided financially for the family and took on responsibility for the fatherless brood. In his time he owned a lot of land around the north.

Harriet's mother was described as a sweet saintly character, the only one in our family tree. She bore her responsibilities with fortitude and never complained. My father remembered her on a Friday, a holy day for many in Ceylon, setting aside vast quantities of food to give to the poor. Crowds would gather around her house even when she was quite frail and elderly. She never disappointed and mobilised her servants and children to provide.

My grandmother had a much older sister but she died young and so her brothers were her friends and constant companions. This may have explained her tomboyish personality, as she never thought or acted much like a girl. She knew herself to be as bright and able as the rest of them and there was nothing that they could do that she could not.

The Handy brothers were outgoing and gregarious. Many had travelled abroad to further their education and went on to become principals and ministers. The youngest son went into medicine and later became a pioneer of cardiology. They also embraced 'western ways' more readily than the demure Sanders clan.

Harriet was an outstanding student at school and was educated in Chundu-kuli College in Jaffna. She then went to the famous Raffles College in Singapore, where she graduated with distinction and completed her senior Cambridge exams with first division in 1922. Sadly the family finances were now running low and as the youngest child it was simply not possible for her to go to university. This was a great disappointment to her. In the end she had to return home and with characteristic resilience taught at Chundukuli, her alma mater.

Ever energetic, she made the best of this and set up the Girl Guide movement there. These organisations may not be so popular now but then they were pivotal in bringing young women together and inspiring them to do more, not only academically but in sport and the cultural aspects of life.

She was thought of as quite foreign in her thinking and shocked the conservative ladies of Jaffna by playing tennis, and that peculiarly British instrument, the piano. How much better for a girl to wear a sari and sit quietly, preferably contemplating religion or whom to marry.

Now here was a problem. Harriet was a girl like no other. She was more than a little unconventional in some ways, far too clever for her own good, had a dead father (that must mean some poor genetics somewhere) and no dowry. Her brothers were not sure what to do with her either.

They hatched a plan, not uncommon in those days, of intermarriage. Her brother was to marry a Susan Sanders. The Sanders family were Christian and educated too, though not well off financially. This also helped with the dowry issue as the Sanders family were not in a position to give much for Susan and so not so much was required from Harriet. The Sanders were country bumpkins however, compared to the polished, better travelled, city loving, Handy family. All were content with this fabulous plan, except for the technicality that Harriet had not agreed to it.

Harriet had been playing a rather exciting game of tennis when she was called to come home. She was in her twenties at this time and quite irritated at the interruption. A rather proper gentleman was seated at the veranda. He was in his thirties and thirteen years her senior, quite elderly in her books. He had sharp features, a moustache, and was tall and lean. Why he was so important, she could not fathom. One thing was for sure, she was certainly not talking to him.

This gentleman then took it upon himself to visit frequently and her brothers seemed most anxious that she should be present on these occasions. It was finally dawning on her what they were up to and she was livid. On each occasion she decided to remain uncharacteristically speechless. Finally the gentleman got fed up, pushing a bunch of flowers into her hands he said, 'I can see I am wasting my time' and started to walk away. At this point she found her voice, purely to appease her family if nothing else. Just as well she did so or thirty one people alive today would not have existed. So it was that my grandparents met.

My grandfather called my grandmother 'Rani'. I never really understood this, as it was not her name. My father explained to me that 'Rani' meant 'queen', and so she was to him. For her it was not what she wanted. Not that she loved anyone else, she had great ideas of the education and the career she might have had.

As always, she adapted. It took time, but she became the college wife. She had parties and entertained in lavish style. She played the piano for school functions, hosted their visitors and taught music and elocution. Unlike her sometimes dour husband, Harriet was a game girl and the life and soul of a party.

She went on to organise the Young Women's Christian Association and lead the Jaffna College choir. She was also the church organist and pianist.

Even when she was an old lady I remember my grandmother at the piano. She had huge hands like a man and could span an octave and three notes. She was most un-granny like and played like a thing possessed.

Though after marriage she earned not a penny, she worked hard and had a brilliant career, albeit linked to her husband's progress. My grandfather took great care of my grandmother and practically fathered her. He was proud of her bright mind and channelled it carefully. They became quite a team. Throughout his working life, she was my grandfather's greatest ally as well as his social convenor.

My aunt Pearl was their first child. I do not really know why but it may have been something to do with pearls making you money. We called her Manie Marmie. She looked like my grandfather but fairly quickly they realised that there was a problem. My aunt had talipes (congenital clubbing) of her foot. This was a blow and they did not know what to do. Today we would not do a lot, perhaps a splint or some physiotherapy.

An eminent foreign surgeon advised surgery. He convinced them that this was the only option, making her handicap even worse. Manie Marmie spent her childhood in callipers but due to her tenacity she walked in spite of all predictions. Unlike today there was no free health care and they paid for this butchery, nor was there recompense for the errors made.

My grandfather had a special place for her, not only as his eldest child but because she was a dutiful, uncomplaining girl. She knew her position and was kind but assertive with her siblings. Such was her insight that she said to her grandmother when she was but a child, 'When you die, will I get your jewels?'

The family moved at some point from Vaddukotia to Nallur. Guru Vasa was given as dowry to my grandmother. It was built by her father and came with a few acres of land. There are tales of C.C. Handy riding a horse and surveying his acres. This was carved up and given to various children. As a result Guru Vasa stood in about two acres. All around were relatives in adjacent bits of property, but our house had the well.

It was a beautiful house and built in the latter part of the nineteenth century. It had a pillared veranda and high ceilings to keep it cool. Inside, wooden beams ran exposed and Italian tiles were imported for the floor and made a lovely multicoloured mosaic design. Two large mahogany doors were at its entrance and a wooden strut was used to shut them at night. All windows had shutters used to keep out the sun and insects. The inner part of the house was used in monsoon season and the outer part in warmer weather.

My grandparents wanted the then 'gentleman's' family of two boys and two girls. They achieved this and my grandmother having given birth, used to painstakingly check each child and later grandchildren for defects. She would literally count fingers and toes, check eyes, ears, nose and so on. After her first child's problems she took little for granted. My father was the last of these four children and so was called *Baba* or baby. Clearly this was not the 'Will of God' as my uncle came along and even though he was technically then the *Baba*, my father continued to be called so.

My father was a mummy's boy and followed her everywhere. He was quite put out by the birth of his brother, particularly because soon after this my grandmother was put into quarantine in a room, as she had contracted chickenpox. He took this as rejection and used to sit on the steps outside her room and chant, 'Once I had a mother, but now she does not talk to me.'

After Manie Marmie came Daniel, named after grandfather's brother. A son was always welcome and ensured the family name was not lost. Daniel was sporty and extrovert but one day, as a teenager when cleaning his ink pen, the nib went into his eye. This effectively punctured it and even the hasty trip to Colombo for surgery could not help him. The eye had to be enucleated due to infection and in its place a cavity formed. How this must have affected a young teenager and his parents, one can only imagine. To make matters worse, for some time a brown prosthetic eye could not be found and he had to make do with a blue one.

I believe that this hideous experience was the making of my uncle. He must have felt a freak, though he was a tall, handsome, lad. In many of the family photographs he is missing or hiding. My uncle and Manie Marmie used to dress with great care, even in later age, and hold themselves with greater poise than their other siblings, who had not been troubled with any debility.

The third child was my aunt Chandra. The last three children all had big eyes and round faces and looked like the Handys. The first two were sharper and more like their father. This aunt was musical like her mother and also played with passion. She later taught at Jaffna College.

Balan, the unexpected baby, came last and was treated with care by his sisters and left behind by his brothers as too small and annoying when they played their many pranks. One day, when my aunts were left in charge,

Balan threw all the drying clothes down the well. His brothers told him that if he did not retrieve them instantly he would be in deep trouble. Poor terrified Balan decided that the best solution was to get his helpful big brothers to lower him down, using the well bucket. They kindly agreed to do this but advised him to pray first, in case he did not make it back. Luckily Manie Marmie spotted him kneeling by the well and put an end to the older siblings' fun.

All activities were centred on the school. The children were often found studying there by day but fully involved in sport and musical activities at night.

My grandmother and a group of college ladies were amazing organisers. They executed plays, musicals and various contests with military precision. The ladies would also arrange elaborate catering and entertainments for a lot of the school's visitors. The school cooks would deal with the mundane and the children's meals.

Ever an experimenter, she would look up recipes for exotic foreign puddings and recreate these or improvise with local ingredients. On one occasion, after the function was over, a large amount of pudding was left and brought back to our home by some well-meaning lady. All the children were delighted, as this was a great treat and puddings at home were too costly to contemplate. They were just about to tuck in when for their bad luck my grandfather came home early from work and went berserk. He sent every bit right back, as he did not want anyone to think that he or his family were profiteering from college events.

Another time upon a visit to our grandparents' when rationing was rife, we wanted to celebrate my father's birthday. Somehow my grandmother got all the ingredients needed but cocoa was impossible to find. Not to be daunted, she got her hands on some protein X, which was a sort of build-up drink for the elderly or sick. She then made this into a topping and it was really quite novel and delicious. We did not share our secret with the neighbours' kids who came to celebrate with us and raved about the unique flavour of the birthday cake.

She was forever buying and storing food away, in case her children or visitors arrived. There were always anniversaries, birthdays or Christmas requiring catering. Our vocation was to find these hiding places and consume all delicacies before some guest got their hands on it. My father and his eldest brother were the worst culprits of all, wiping out entire family supplies in one sitting.

Harriet was a prize negotiator and dealt with all the vendors who regularly turned up. To this day I can never bargain and feel very awkward doing so but she was very astute and got the best price from the fish man, vegetable man, barber or anyone else who turned up at home regularly. All these vendors knew she had a sharp eye and would not be palmed off with anything but the best. It was a game and usually ended with a good gossip about what was going on in the neighbourhood. If she needed something they did not have, she and the servants would go to market.

She also had to contend with the servants stealing, so it was all quite a challenge for her. My father had sent some expensive brandy from abroad that she kept locked in her *almera*. This was only to come out on special occasions and to be consumed when important guests arrived. The servants however managed to get the *almera* open and regularly sipped away at the stuff but were careful to top up with water. One Christmas evening Harriet grandly opened her foreign bottle and dished out its watery contents to her visitors. They were greatly disappointed, declaring that French brandy was definitely overrated.

My grandparents' house was always full of relatives, children, grandchildren, nieces and nephews. When one of her brothers was evacuated from Malaysia during the Second World War, his family came to stay a while. Nothing fazed my grandmother; she catered cheerfully for all and was once described as the ultimate hostess, charming, fun and wonderfully inventive. In stark contrast to my grandfather, she aimed to put people at ease.

She would write long letters to all her extended family and when we came to Britain we used to wait eagerly for her informative and entertaining updates. We would all gather around my father and he would read and re-read these to us. In those days, we could not phone our grandparents and having lived with them, this was the only contact we had for years. We used to rush downstairs in the morning in the hope of receiving news.

It must have been a bit of a shock to my grandmother to inherit us when my parents left Ceylon. Although my grandfather had agreed to this, the bulk of the work involved fell on her shoulders. We were then aged nine, five and two; my grandmother was sixty five and grandfather seventy eight! I think we exhausted them but we also gave them life and had a special parent/grandparent relationship because of this. My brother thought Harriet was his mother, even though he was often told that this was not the case. He once said to our mother, 'You seem like a nice lady but I want my mummy', and then started to scream.

Now everyone knew that I was 'pining' for my parents. That was true but I also knew that all I had to do was stand by my parents' picture near the piano and cry and sooner or later grandma would be crying too and *Vimto* and *bulto* (a type of toffee) would be sent for. There was a shop just across from the house which was a great source of consolation to me and more than made up for my 'orphaned' status. The old man who ran it was delighted with the steady flow of consumption from Sanders master's grandchildren.

Even after retirement, my grandparents were fully involved with the church and all the local activities. My grandmother was skinny and hyperactive in those days and never sat down for long.

She was forever attending some function or other and her *almera* had a vast collection of saris, matching blouses and handbags, in every shade of the rainbow, to facilitate this. We loved to feel the different fabrics – Benaris silk, Indian cotton, crepe georgette and bags made of metal from a bygone age. We also sneaked a peak at her personal letters and accidentally made reference one day to some family dispute we were not supposed to know about, sending her into a panic.

When my grandfather had a heart attack and other health issues, they made brief trips to Colombo for the best medical care but always came home as soon as possible.

When finally my grandfather died we received a letter from my grandmother detailing how she had closed the shutters and doors of our house for the first time in her life, this being Iyah's job. The bar was placed over the double doors of Guru Vasa. She then sat on packing crates and said that in her mind's eye she saw images of their life together. They had been married for fifty five years. He was her salt, something essential to her life. Their children had done so well and their marriage, which had such a tenuous start, had been a success. The next chapter she had to face alone.

All my cousins thought of Guru Vasa as their holiday home. We have travelled the world and stayed in so many places but this was our special place, full of memories and epitomised 'our golden days'.

After this she travelled the world to spend time with her children, first to Colombo, Zambia, Scotland, Hawaii and finally to Australia. She was staying in Colombo when the riots broke out in 1983. A car was sent to evacuate her and she refused to move. She had the presence of mind to run around the garden of my uncle's home, collecting our family photographs, shoving them into her handbag. If not for this single act, we would have no pictorial record of our lives there. I still have a photograph of my grandfather in his teaching robes burnt at the corners. It would be so easy to have this air brushed out like the other pictures, but I keep it so, to remember her bravery.

She later came to Scotland and stayed with us when I was studying for my history exam and challenged me when I said George IV was mad. 'Wrong!' she barked. 'It was George III and he had porphyria.' This without text books or any reference.

I used to go to the library every week for her and get large print books. Within six months she had read their entire collection and was getting bored. She always felt most useful when she stayed in Australia with Manie Marmie who used to say, 'Ammah is my legs and I am her eyes.'

Harriet had favourites. You knew pretty quickly if you were or were not. My aunt held a party for her once and she hugged some people lovingly and ignored others. My cousin challenged her and said, 'Appammah, you really cannot do this.'

'At my age I can do anything I want' was the reply.

I went to visit her in Australia after I had married and she was most interested in my choice. My husband was introduced to the vast clan of relatives who had escaped civil war and gone to settle there. One of Harriet's nieces said to my husband, 'Welcome to the Handy family.'

'I can barely cope with the Sanders family,' was his response!

My uncle Daniel was then the dean at the University of Illinois and was planning to retire and move to Australia too, to look after her. He was lecturing in San Francisco and, a little tired, retreated to his hotel room. He was a man of regular habit and always phoned his wife, my aunt Chelvathy at specific times. When he did not, she demanded the door be broken down and he was found fully suited sitting on his chair, dead.

My grandmother was never the same after that. I heard her talking to my father over the phone and she said, *'Aiyo Baba Endai chinnai kurruvi paranthitithai.'* Hard to exactly translate Tamil but it means, 'My tiny fledgling has flown the nest.' She stopped talking much after this and then became muddled.

There is video footage of these later years which I hate to see: my sister, visiting Australia, trying to jog my grandmother's memory of her favourite songs, without much success.

*Where is my wondering boy tonight?*
*The boy of my tenderest care*
*The boy that was once my joy and light,*
*The child of my love and prayer?*
*Oh where is my boy tonight?*
*Oh where is my boy tonight?*
*My heart o'er flows, for I love him he knows;*
*Oh where is my boy tonight?*

Robert Lowry

It is to our family's eternal shame that she ended her days in a nursing home in Australia. Both her daughters had fallen ill and my father had suffered a stroke. She had become befuddled, less mobile and incontinent. She died within months of being admitted. I can remember begging my husband that we go and get her. Of course he said no, we already had my father's illness to contend with and she was thousands of miles away.

She had brought us all up and was devoted to her children and grand-children. How could we let this happen? I wish those last days had never been. I wish that I could have wiped them out entirely.

# CHAPTER 5

# APPAH

My grandparents' children, as I have already mentioned, were generally tall and fair. Every litter has its runt however, and my father (at birth at least) was the small, dark one. One of my great-aunts was so horrified that she said, '*Aiyoo! Ivan karuppu*', which translates as 'My goodness, this one is black!'

On the plus side for Harriet, he was the double of her father. She never vocalised this but it mattered to her. Of course if your father was a bright, well known, heroic figure, who you barely knew, this was bound to matter.

I visited my dad's cousin once and was bemused as to why she had a large picture of my father in graduation robes on her piano. I even wondered if she had been soft on him, when she said abruptly, 'That is your great-grandfather, not your father.'

Having already caused concern with his colour, which was sure to have him labelled as a peasant's son, he went on to develop allergies to all sorts of things, especially sea foods, which is what we consumed in large volume. The Ceylonese love their fish, crab, prawns and squid. Here lay the main source of protein and the consumption of chicken and mutton was a rare treat.

He followed Harriet around, as if he was her shadow and he could do no wrong in her eyes. My grandfather, spotting this, was extra harsh to compensate.

37

She would cook all manner of delicacies to make up for the poor boy's allergies. He could not bear to be left out of what the others were eating however and when no one was watching, helped himself to little morsels. Thus he desensitised himself and ended up secretly gorging on double portions. Needless to say he did not remain the runt of the litter for long. Nothing could be done about the colour, and his big brother, when irritated by him, would call him 'Blackie!'

My grandparents were ahead of their time in the level of knowledge they had on dietary issues and each child was fed volumes of milk, eggs, vegetables and vast quantities of protein. Since my grandfather kept goats and chickens, milk and eggs were in great supply for all the family and many of the vegetables were grown on site. Favourites were a fried aubergine curry, mallum made from leeks and coconut and daal. On the grounds of Guru Vasa alone drumstick, pawpaw, mango, lemons, limes, coconuts and bananas grew in ample supply. All the children assisted in the 'farming' of these garden treats. Although naughty, Dad could be helpful and sweet to his parents too.

My father was very fond of both his sisters and carried their bags and generally ran little errands for them. My aunt Chandra used to have piano lessons at their grandfather C.C. Handy's old home and he would walk with her, carrying her music books, wait patiently till her lessons were over and then walk her back. He did this even at university with my aunt Manie Marmie when she went on her mammoth shopping trips and she always paid him back with an ice cream.

His main companion however, was Daniel. They were the gruesome twosome and got into every scrape imaginable. Daniel was always smart enough to evade blame and Dad got it every time. The pair were well known trouble makers and were walking home from school one day, stones and sling in hand. One of these stones accidentally hit a classmate and before they could blink her mother was round complaining that Dad had tried to assault her child. He narrowly missed a smack, as another neighbour witnessed what had happened and stopped my grandfather from punishing him.

Another escapade was trying to race around the district with the dobbie's bullock cart, when he came to uplift the laundry. They were always trying to run away somewhere and as voracious readers got a lot of their ideas from books; *Robinson Crusoe* was a favourite. They were secretly embarking on building a raft when spotted by their cousin Charlie Handy. He wanted to join in and they were not for it. Charlie was so annoyed that he got his revenge by telling Iyah. They were just about to cast off on an adventure, when they were reeled in for retribution.

They sat in church behind a family of boys and enjoyed regularly knocking them on the head. Each boy thought this was their father reprimanding them and the poor lads would sit and sob quietly, whilst the wicked Sanders boys stifled giggles.

It was quite a challenge for my grandfather to have such an unruly child in his school, so when his son was badly behaved he made a point of making an example of him and inflicting swift punishment.

One day, when Dad was a teenager, he said to my grandfather, 'You keep caning me but it is not making a difference.' My grandfather never caned him again. It had to be remembered that in those days the belt was quite in vogue in schools and it could be argued that we have gone too much the other way nowadays and that children lack discipline and guidance.

Even late into his teens, Dad would sit at my grandmother's feet and follow her about. When he went on a scouting trip he was given pocket money to spend on himself. He hoarded every penny and then utilised the lot on a gift for her instead. His bad behaviour caused her amusement and they shared a love of music and literature. Even she could not get him to play the piano though and she once got uncharacteristically irritated with his attempts and rapped him on the knuckles with a ruler. In response to this he gave up altogether. Sport was much more interesting for him and he was forever out with his friends.

He did well in his studies, achieving the best marks with minimal effort. At prizegiving he used to get a friend to come up to the podium with him, to help carry his books. He loved mathematics best of all and was keen to study this at university. Careers advice was simple then and if you got straight As you did medicine. His mother was very keen to for him to emulate his famous cardiologist uncle and he reluctantly gave in.

At this point, my grandparents already had two children at Colombo University and were paying fees and subsistence. They were happy to make all the necessary financial sacrifices however, to facilitate their son's success. He was packed off on the Jaffna to Colombo train with a bag full of eats and treats, lovingly prepared by my grandmother, and a term's fees.

When he arrived at the other side he was met by Daniel, who was already well established and one of the 'cool chaps' at university.

'First, don't tell anyone you are related to me and if they ask you, say you drink,' he advised.

Freshmen were fairly quickly introduced to ragging at university in the fifties and as predicted Dad was asked,

'Do you drink?'

'Yes,' he responded.

'What is your choice?'

'I'll take a pint of arrack.'

Arrack is a cheap, revolting spirit, distilled from the coconut tree, drunk in Ceylon, not unlike methylated spirit. It is never had in anything but small quantities but the naïve northern freshman who had never tasted alcohol in his life was not to know this. He was lucky that he did not end up in casualty, having his stomach pumped. He was super fit at that time and when he finished school was the captain of the basketball team. This probably saved him and he got the reputation of being a hard man overnight. Quite a transformation for a mummy's boy.

Ragging started off being a bit of fun but could turn nasty. Dad took in his stride commands like, 'Lie on the grass and swim like a fish for a few hours.' He was also famously asked to emulate the statue of David at the university gates. When big brother walked past his sibling in his birthday suit he was asked, 'Is that yokel related to you?'

'I don't know who the bugger is,' was the emphatic reply.

Fairly soon after arriving at university, Dad declared himself to be a vegetarian. This was an old trick so that he could get special meals again and, when no one was watching, eat all the non-veg food as well.

He was also quickly introduced to horse racing and happily spent many hours at the racecourse with his new friends. Being a mathematician at heart he decided that winning at the races was easy. All you needed to do was double your bets every time you lost and eventually when you won you would be in profit. This assumes that the races are not rigged, so he learnt the hard way and lost a term's fees.

My poor grandfather received a telegram for more funds. I would have loved to have seen his face and heard his expletives. Dad did feel guilty and soon got a job and posted the money back. He received a letter by return of post with all the money intact and a note to say that he was at university to study, not to earn.

He did not repeat the success he had in school at medical college. He really did not want to be there and decided not to attend lectures. He was blessed with the ability to forge signatures and so proceeded to sign himself off as completing labs and course work without doing a day's work. His cardiologist uncle knew there was foul play afoot but had no way of finding out how he did it and no concrete proof.

He hung about with the lads who were no hopers and a girl called Whinnie. Whinnie sat near him from the start and she too was tall and black. She was quite a tomboy by all accounts. She was very fond of him and vice versa. Yet in his head she was simply one of the boys and he never thought of her in any other way. Poor Whinnie.

He also briefly lodged with a Burgher (Eurasian) family. The landlady had a beautiful married daughter whose husband was away with the army. The landlady was always happy to take the rent but treated her lodgers badly. Her daughter, in contrast, was very kind to him and swapped her delicious cooked breakfasts for his bread. He did not lodge there long and eventually the husband came back. In short, he was entirely naïve about girls and happy to observe. He had enough wit to know that although he got into a lot of scrapes, girls were different; they were a dangerous species that could get him into deep strife. He knew his limits and was cautious with his affections.

The medical students at Brodie Hostel were known to be a rum lot. They were forever in trouble with the police but too clever to get caught. There seemed to be an on-going battle to outwit and irritate anyone involved with law enforcement.

Fun things to do on a Saturday night included gathering en masse by the road into Colombo city and crossing and re-crossing the main road. They ended up backing up the traffic for miles and causing a public nuisance. What can you say to, 'But officer we're only crossing the road'?

Another source of amusement was negotiating which male medical student most looked like a girl and dressing him up accordingly. This lad would then be left standing looking vulnerable under a tree or in front of some foliage. Sooner or later some fool would stop by to proposition the lonely maiden, only to have a bunch of oafs jump out and beat him up.

The boys used to play cards until the small hours and rummy and poker were favourites. One of his friends had a granny in town, who smoked and drank and would beat the boys mercilessly at every game. However much they begged her she never returned the money they lost.

At the weekends his other pastimes included horse racing, cards, drinking, boxing and playing billiards, often all night long. No one ever expected him to get through medical school. One of his fellow students saw him sleeping on the billiard table the day before his finals and said, 'Sanders is a loser, he is sure to fail.' Interestingly the speaker did so, and Dad just scraped through.

He made great friends at university. He hung out with Sinhalese, Tamil and Burgher boys and kept in touch with many of them until the end of his life. He would often say that the Tamil medical students were too studious and preferred his fun loving, easy going Sinhalese friends.

His doctor uncle felt the boy was a disgrace and was up to every trick. How could he have completed his course work and passed having barely attended? He complained to my grandparents but they were miles away and there was little that they could do.

Meanwhile Manie Marmie had a string of suitors after her, whilst studying sciences at university. She worked her charm on them all but both brothers were quick to put off any men they felt unsuitable. There was a dapper, bright, engineering student by the name of Herbert whom they hounded less than the others. He soon became a favourite of the brothers, enjoying and partaking in many of their escapades.

I am reminded of the scene in a movie called *My Big Fat Greek Wedding*, when the brother says to the sister's suitor something like, 'You like my sister, it's good. She likes you. We like you. You hurt my sister, we kill you.' I wonder what would have happened if they liked Herbert less.

If you passed out well in medical school you went on to get a job in a prestigious Colombo hospital. If you passed out badly you were sent out to the wilderness. Dad was posted to a backwater town called Kankesanthurai (KKS). He could not have cared less and looked forward to an easier pace of life. He had enjoyed medical school but the time had come to move on and he was acutely aware of the financial burden that he was placing on his parents.

Every six months newly graduated doctors would arrive in KKS hospital and the phones in the nurses living quarters would ring nonstop. The verdict was that this time two had arrived, a gentle looking, fine featured small guy and a *thrada* (big guy).

Dad strolled into the wards with his stethoscope around his neck and a bulge at his hip where his cigarettes were kept in a tin. Within days of arriving he spotted the most beautiful girl he had ever seen. She was built like a miniature Maureen O'Hara, attractive and spirited. The nurses' uniforms in the fifties were very complimentary to the female form, unlike the sack-like outfits of today. He stood no chance at all. She felled him like a tree.

In one of his more sentimental moments, my brother once said 'My father was a God and my mother was an angel.' I think I would modify that to 'My father was a God and my mother certainly had the face of an angel.' Poor Dad. From that moment on my father's life was never to be the same again.

He used to say that the mustard seed was small but grows to a very large tree. People underestimate the power of the mustard seed. So it was with my mother. She was a little vision in high heels, curly long black hair, with a laugh that was infectious and almost too loud. Only a fool would misjudge the mustard seed and as Dad was no fool, he got the full measure of my mother.

CHAPTER 6

# THE MOST BEAUTIFUL GIRL IN THE WORLD

If you ever hear a name that is completely unpronounceable, it is highly likely that you are dealing with someone from Ceylon. Can you imagine being called Mangai Saravanamuthu. Even I am never sure that I'm spelling or saying my mother's name right. The other habit that Ceylonese have, is that you can be called different names by different people. Dad was Baba to his family, Sandy to some friends, Sanders to work colleagues and Sam in Scotland. This custom of different names for different people, comes back to haunt me each Christmas. My mother is forgetful these days and so I dutifully assist her with her Christmas cards. It is a form of annual torture to be endured, as she sends about two hundred of these and the 'tos' and 'froms' vary constantly. I am not sure who I am writing to, or whether the person receiving the card has any idea whom it is from.

If my father's family were all establishment, education and prim and proper, my mother's family were not. My maternal grandmother married the love of her life and had a daughter, Nesi. Unfortunately, her first husband then died and she settled for my grandfather. This was an entirely pragmatic arrangement, as my grandfather too was widowed. The couple went on to have my mother, my uncle Rajathurai and my aunt Ranee. Though the eldest was technically my mother's half-sister, my mother was devoted to Nesi and vice versa. This was partly due to the ten year age gap with her other siblings.

My maternal grandfather was always full of compliments about his first wife and would annoy my grandma, by telling her that my mother's lush curly locks reminded him of wife number one. He was the good looking one, with fine features and much charm. His weakness was that he was not wise in his management of business matters and was regularly swindled by his own brother.

My maternal grandmother was the stronger partner in the relationship; she ran the family and faced all adversity stoically. She came from a wealthier family and her in-laws found her to be stuck up and distant. Her main reason for maintaining this stance was that she could not bear to see her husband being repeatedly cheated by his younger brother and sisters. This brother even cuckolded him into signing over the deeds to some of his land. Many years later my mother came to hear of this and sweetly asked my grand uncle if she could purchase some property back from him. My grand-uncle was happy to sell and she was required to pay an exorbitant sum, to which she readily agreed. The documents were drawn up and signed for but she subsequently refused to pay a penny. He was incensed and ranted at her, but she simply ignored him for the rest of his life and felt that he had his justice.

The family owned rice and paddy fields. They managed financially but were not well off. My aunt Nesi also spent a lot of her time with my great-grandmother who poured affection and funds on her, as a fatherless child. This irritated my mother beyond belief as she thought it unfair. She could not understand the difference between them but my grandparents were grateful for this financial and emotional support.

My great-grandmother was always careful to visit her grandchildren when her husband was not around. She and my great-grandfather remained married but lived separately and disliked each other intensely. Neither married again, as they were so put off by their experience with each other.

My mother has many tales of the hardship they faced and she always ends these stories with, 'You children have no idea, sometimes there was little food. We were always served first as the children and my parents would do without.' I have seen photographs of my mother as a girl, so I find this hard to believe. She had two thick black plaits and was bursting out of her school uniform.

Ammah (Mum) spent a lot of time with her little brother but was not averse to beating him up if he annoyed her. In one of her famous fits of temper she threw a tin at him and he had to be taken to casualty and stitched up.

Ranee was ten years younger and as such did not qualify as a childhood playmate. My grandfather pampered his children and my grandmother was the hand of discipline. She took responsibility for most matters for he was more of a social butterfly.

My grandfather became unwell suffering a series of strokes from a young age. I can now recognise that he probably had cerebral amyloid, which is a slowly progressive, dementing disease. I remember him as a sweet, cheerful, old gentleman, who seemed perpetually on the cusp of death, for all the time I knew him.

Even from a young age, my mother received a lot of attention, as she looked like a miniature Maureen O'Hara. She is always keen to mention that she did not court this, in the same way that my father did not court trouble. My grandmother decided that the most prudent course of action would be to remove her to Koppai Christian College. This was a boarding school and would give her an excellent education and take her far away from the stares and comments of the local lads, which may have proved to be too much of a temptation for her.

The Christian schools were better run than the Hindu ones but my mother was very secure in her Hindu faith, even as a young girl, so my grandmother did not worry too much about this. As my grandfather became sicker, this time with malaria, paying the fees became a challenge but my aunt Nesi was earning by then and as usual paid for my mother and saved the day.

Ammah did not mind boarding and enjoyed the challenge of her new environment. She was outgoing and friendly like her father and quickly established herself in the 'in crowd'. This may have included bullying a few of the less extrovert girls, but such was life.

She went home regularly at weekends and did well in her exams. Her family was keen for her to qualify as a teacher or study something at college. She was proud even as a child and felt the need to work as soon as possible and not be a burden to them.

Meanwhile Nesi had qualified as a midwife and became an invaluable help financially as well as becoming something of the village heroine. She was a self-less character, who would do anything for those she knew, including relatives, friends and patients, but could also be very sharp and stood no nonsense.

She was pathologically generous and when I was a child she gave me a gold ring, which she could ill afford to buy. In my usual absent minded way, I left it on the window ledge when washing my hands and she was livid when she discovered it. I was so upset by my carelessness and her annoyance, that I have stuck to fake jewellery ever since.

My aunt Nesi then did something quite extraordinary. Whilst pursuing her midwifery rounds she had met a Buddhist, Sinhalese, police sergeant and declared that she was marrying him. Her family was aghast and could not understand her choice. Living and working in the north, with very few Sinhalese and many Tamil men all around, this was simply bizarre and an all-out effort to make life more complicated than necessary.

My mother adored her would be brother-in-law Wicky. They could only communicate in English as he could not speak Tamil. She thought the whole thing hugely romantic and my grandmother had to give in, as no one else seemed to be seeing any sense. Everyone thought Nesi would move to Colombo or Galle from whence Wicky came but both remained firmly in Mathagal for their entire married life. Given what happened later in Sri Lanka, this was remarkable.

Wicky was a kind soul and took on the role of fathering his wife's family, as his father-in-law was so frail and brother and sisters-in-law were considerably younger than him. He constantly encouraged all of them, especially my mother to study and further their education. He promised to support them financially for as long as was needed.

All of this advice fell on deaf ears. My mother thought it dreadful that the young couple was burdened with this responsibility. Encouraged by her cousin Nadarajah she signed up as a nurse for the TB ward. In the fifties TB was still a major killer and effective antibiotics had just made their appearance. There was big money to be made doing this job, so long as you did not contract TB yourself or die. The added advantage was that you could study and earn at the same time, hence no need for dependency and, in Ammah's case, there was every opportunity to send money home.

There was only one big hitch to this clever plan. You had to be eighteen to sign up and she was sixteen. This would have put most people off but not so my mother or her mad cousin. I am not sure how they did it but they procured a fake birth certificate. To this day there is great confusion about my mother's date of birth. If ever I am asked I just don't know what to say, as a number of legal documents still have this old date. People then look at me as if I was some sort of imbecile or worse still thoroughly callous. How bad is your relationship with your parent, if you don't even know their date of birth? The other explanation is that she is probably way older than Dad and that this was an elaborate tale to put us off the shocking truth.

My maternal grandparents were now both giving up and allowing their children to do whatever they wanted. They seemed to have lost control altogether. My daughter is sixteen and I find it hilarious when mum tries to warn her about the dangers of the outside world and encourages her to be cautious. If only she knew what the giver of the advice got up to. A clear case of, 'Do as I say, not as I do.'

The nurses' uniforms were fabulous. They had starched white aprons with enormous hats, silver buckles and white shoes with heels. Ammah looked and felt amazing. She quickly made friends with a girl called Benjamin (everyone used surnames). Benjamin was a bit wild and quite bossy but on the plus side, really looked after her friends and showed them the ropes. If you weren't her friend, life could become difficult.

Nursing was a rewarding job financially and emotionally. Attendants and auxiliaries did the unpleasant bits of personal care, so there was a lot of holding hands, giving of meals, injections and, best of all, assisting doctor. The master plan was to study as much as possible and ultimately become a matron, so long as no distractions came along!

Dad was posted to KKS for twelve months. It was hard work but he enjoyed it – better than studying – and when he was off he fished, swam, played basketball and indulged in bird watching.

This bird was of the human variety and quite a feisty little creature. She hung out with some of the wildest nurses in the residency and he was cautious, if not a little suspicious of her. She could be very sweet if she liked you but he noted with interest habits like dragging the patient's arm towards the needle, if she was not so fond of them. There was also another nurse in the hospital called Mangai who was, by all accounts, a bit lecherous, hence separating who did what was a challenge.

At this point my mother had a dental problem and was forced to see the hospital dentist who was thought to be a total womaniser. She took an orderly with her, as she was very reluctant to be alone with this unpleasant man. The dentist was one step ahead and sent the orderly away on a useless errand.

He then kissed my poor defenceless mother. She literally jumped out of her chair and ran as fast as she could, in her three inch heels. It was her first kiss and she was deeply upset that he had stolen it. The beastly man then spread the story of his irresistible charms all around the hospital and even boasted to Dad.

After five months of standing at the entrance of the ward smoking (ah, the good old days), and watching, Dad finally started talking to my mother. Apparently he tried to help her study on nightshift and then they started meeting for coffee. Benjamin was furious. She and father had a mutual and instant dislike of one another. She was already going out with another doctor but bizarrely felt that Mum was making a fool of herself and that my father's intentions were dishonourable.

Dad advised my mother not to tell anyone about their relationship and not to discuss it. I would think this very suspicious but a girl's reputation at that time could be lost simply with gossip.

It wasn't long before Dad was posted to Thalaimannar and mum was left alone. He phoned and wrote constantly but all the hospital staff laughed at the foolish, pretty nurse who thought she had caught a doctor and was then dumped.

Dad wanted a little time on his own to be sure of what he was going to do next. My favourite picture of my father is sitting at the end of the pier in Thalaimannar fishing. This was his time for contemplation. The Indian Ocean is a bit unsettled and his white flannels are blowing in the wind. It all looks idyllic but, my island in the sun, it never was, was it? Fishing was banned for some peculiar reason and was only allowed if you had a permit, which he did not. His friends told him that if he kept flouting police rules, one day they would push him into the sea. I wonder, what he was thinking as he fished? The stormy sea reflects his inner state. Harriet would not have been happy to have my mother as a daughter-in-law.

Doctors in Ceylon were regarded as a fabulous catch. Most did private practice and had huge earning potential. It was common to expect a hefty dowry on marriage, or at least marry a young lady whose relatives could set you up in a lucrative practice.

The Saravanamuttus had no money and no contacts. They were the right caste but they were Hindu and Dad's family was deeply Christian, as already mentioned. Mummy's darling was about to break her heart.

When my father phoned the hospital, switchboard used to tap his calls and have a great laugh at the couple's expense. My mother had to endure sarcastic comments and her friendship with Benjamin reached an all-time low. She must have felt isolated and vulnerable but to her credit, for once she spoke little and got on with her work. She trusted him and waited quietly to see what would happen next.

She took a train journey home and en-route a car was noted to be driving in parallel. Trains were slower then and when she peeked out of the coach window, she saw Dad. When the train stopped at the station he jumped in and gave her ice cream. Another time on her birthday he ordered an enormous cake from Cargils, which was then a famous department store, like Jenners in Edinburgh. Some of these tales got back to the anxious grandparents on both sides.

After one year my father decided that this really was the girl for him but religious differences bothered him. He was keen to present a unified, firm foundation for any would-be children. My mother decided to convert to the Christian faith and was baptised with the Christian name Irene. Ice cream and cake were all very well, but at this point I would have had difficulty.

My aunt Ranee once contemptuously told my mother that if Dad said 'thai' she would say 'thay'. I think these are bharatanatyam dance moves that complement each other but what she meant was that my mother was losing herself so much, that she would basically do anything Dad said. What had happened to her devout, regular attendance at the temple?

This statement completely misjudged my mother. She adored and trusted my father, there was literally nothing that she would not do for him and vice versa. She had her reservations about it all but trusted that he would do her no harm. Christianity was also a monotheistic, relatively intolerant faith. Hindus believed in the many faces of God. In Ceylon they were more tolerant, so that long before my mother met my Christian father, she often attended church and Buddhist temples with Wicky. She had also been educated in a Christian school and had a good idea of what it all entailed.

She loved the rituals of her faith. She loved the colours and festivals, which even I remember as a child. The temples themselves were so exquisitely carved and painted in vibrant shades and bursting with life. The Anglican Church was a sober affair. It must have been like switching from colour television to black and white.

51

When a couple first start courting and in the lead up to marriage there is often a bit of mental bartering that goes on. How will this relationship play out? Who will do what? How much does each give in to the other? How much of yourself do you lose when you become one? It was never like this with my parents. They flowed together like two tributaries of the Mahaweli Ganga (famous Sri Lankan river) into the wide Indian Ocean, naturally and without effort.

My mother attended Confirmation classes and was christened into the Protestant faith.

Meanwhile Harriet sent a posse to the hospital to find out more about 'the girl'. The report back was dire. They said that she had liaisons with several men, including the hospital dentist, and her reputation was in tatters. My mother was on leave when the posse arrived and their reports were based on the other Mangai. Dad was furious with his mother and in her lack of faith in him and his judgement.

He met his would be in-laws, who liked him instantly but were worried about what his family would say and how they would treat my mother.

They had already inherited one Sinhalese in-law with great reluctance but he had turned out to be a gem, so they were more flexible in their thinking than the deeply conservative Sanders side.

My *Marma* (Mum's brother), was playing up in a big way and not studying and my aunt Ranee had disgraced the family by entering and winning a beauty contest. Mum's features were finer than Ranee's, but the latter had the height, a wonderful figure and poise. Though Tamil she was dressed in national Sinhala costume for the contest, not a swim suit, I hasten to add. My grandparents were disgusted, however, at the thought of strangers staring at her and commenting on her face, form et cetera. They were now forced to go with the flow and their feelings of disempowerment grew stronger on a daily basis.

Wicky and Nesi tried to do what they could to improve the situation and exert discipline but they had their own children and full time jobs to contend with.

Today all this seems a bit over the top, as people intermarry with ease, and the world, with travel, is a smaller place. In the fifties, in Ceylon, people like my parents were rebels and threatened the fabric of society. Castes, different religions and different nationalities aspired to keep each to their own. In reality, however, the islanders were a mixed bag. I often remind my own children that I am a thoroughbred and that they are mongrels. They tell me that mongrels are fitter and brighter than in-breds!

Finally, my mother was taken to Guru Vasa to meet the in-laws. My grandfather, true to form, drew on the pros and cons of their situation but accepted Dad's choice. He was ever the supporter of the underdog. The others were too well mannered and courteous to make any comment. They were also wary as Dad, when crossed, had a fearsome temper. My grandmother was devastated.

The wedding date was set and all concerned decided that it was to be a small family affair. My aunt Chandra was due to have her baby at any moment and could not attend. Manie Marmie coiffured my mother's hair and my aunt Chelavthy (Daniel's wife) was in charge of the flowers. Nesi and Wicky did everything else.

The bride arrived in time and the groom's car skidded so he was late. The mother-in-law howled. The guests numbered more than the invites, as uninvited people turned up to see the fun.

I have often wondered why this was so and why my mother seemed to have people wishing her ill. It is only supposition but perhaps they thought she was getting above her station. Her relationship and subsequent break up with Nurse Benjamin would have also contributed to this. In the end I think some people were simply jealous of her and envious of her beauty.

Dad's favourite film star was Ava Gardner. He had a massive poster of her in his room when he was a medical student. I once read her biography and she was a wild creature. What was interesting is that her great natural beauty was a gift and a curse. She too made women jealous, just by being her and attracted the wrong sort of men. There was also the assumption that because she was so stunning, she was brainless. Until then it had never occurred to me that being beautiful could be destructive and not an asset.

I detest my parents' wedding pictures. They both look very stressed and unnatural. My maternal grandfather, for once, took responsibility and advised my mother that what she was doing was quite serious and that she was not to laugh in her usual too loud fashion. The result of this is that she looks like she could have done with a shot of ECT. My father was defiant as ever but not happy.

Well, it was only one day in their lives and soon over. My father said 'Don't worry about it. I'm marrying you, not my mother.' So on that day, having changed her faith and abandoned a lot that was familiar, Mangai Saravanamuthu was gone and Irene Sanders emerged.

# CHAPTER 7

# LOVE IS A MANY SPLENDORED THING

There was a movie famous in the fifties, that was a favourite with my parents called, *Love is a Many Splendored Thing*. It starred the late William Holden and Jennifer Jones. It made quite a statement in its day. Set in Hong Kong in 1949, it was about a Eurasian doctor who fell in love with an American war correspondent. That in itself was bad enough and pushed the boundaries, but to add to this he was also unhappily married. She loses her reputation and compromises her career by going out with him, then he dies. She is left standing under a tree reflecting on their love, which was a many spendored thing.

I would have called the movie *Love Can Be a Very Destructive Thing*. I'm sure she would have become professor of paediatrics, had she not shocked everyone by going out with a married man. He upset all his friends and associates, not to mention his poor wife, wherever she was, by mixing with a 'coloured' girl. If he had not been so enamoured, he may have paid more attention to the bomb that was about to drop on his head.

After getting married my parents went to Guru Vasa and briefly to Mathagal, my mother's family home, where they were given two gold sovereigns in traditional Hindu style. There was a welcoming ceremony with blessings, *pottus*, garlands, a *thali* with various auspicious things placed on it and incense.

It was all very short and sweet, after which they went on to Thaliamannar where Dad worked.

There the party really began. Dad's friend, Sinnathurai, who was the village teacher, hailed them before they approached and insisted that they change back into their wedding attire. On arrival the people had gathered to greet the newlyweds who were garlanded again and a party was thrown in their honour. There were speeches and presents as Dad was well known and liked as the medical officer in that area. It was quite some gathering and my parents really enjoyed themselves and valued the gesture.

One of the reasons for Dad's popularity was that he was quite relaxed about payment from his patients. There was a very basic sort of NHS and government funding, but most doctors charged their patients for anything above this. If you worked in Colombo you could become quite wealthy and if you worked in a poorer area, less so. Because my father made a vocation of not excelling himself, he usually ended up in the middle of nowhere. Even so he could have done alright; except for the fact that throughout his life he never did one day of private practice. He felt that health care should be equally available to all. This was an extraordinary stance to take, given that most doctors in Ceylon then had thriving private practices. His own family had some of the richest doctors on the island.

His poor patients felt bad about this, so they would cook him food or gift him a chicken. By the time my mother arrived at the doctor's bungalow, it was overrun by poultry, two huge dogs and a belligerent servant boy, who was delighted to have a doctor who did not care. She was positively revolted by the mess and set about organising the servant boy and cleaning the place.

She had never cooked in her life and her burnt offerings got too much for Dad, so his first gift to her, which I now have, was every new bride's Bible; *The Daily News Cookery Book*. The servant boy thought it hilarious that he was being instructed by a novice, who kept consulting her book. The chickens kept pecking my mother for she no longer allowed them in the house and the dogs gnashed their teeth, showing their displeasure.

She was not naturally a good cook but with sheer determination she went to task and learned to boil rice and make *parrupu* and mutton curry. The basics having been mastered she then incinerated a number of vegetables but was always good at *mallum*, Dad's favourite. This was a dish that my siblings and I came to detest because it was served up with monotonous regularity. It is a bit like a stir fry with onions and leeks. I think Ceylonese meats, sea foods and starches are fabulous but when it comes to vegetables, they are cremated beyond recognition. I could eat chicken, mutton, prawns, crab, squid, fish curry, *pittu, hoppers, thosia, iddili* and rice to my heart's content, but anything green and curried was given a miss. My sweet tooth is also more than catered for in Scotland. In Ceylon, fifty per cent of the time, dessert is likely to be fruits and ice cream. You got the odd *vatillupum* or *payasam* but they, too, were generally worth missing. If you have the gut space, I recommend you fill it with more sea foods or meat.

In the end, Mum did become a good cook. In fact, love being a very splendid thing, the pair of them sat around eating and entertaining. Dad gave up much of his sport as this was too much time spent away from Mum; going to work was bad enough. Mum cooked double portions for Dad, because she loved him so. He ate them as he did not want to upset her and doubled in size. She looked the same, so presumably did not consume what she was shovelling into him. I blame my tendency to overeat on my mother. She did not naturally like cooking but did it for love. She then expected you to eat double for love. Being a dutiful child I was always happy to oblige.

My mother wanted four children, preferably two boys and two girls. They moved to Badulla, tea plantation country in the central part of the island, for his next transfer and mum started to get quite sick. She had hyperemesis and the vomiting did not stop, blighting her entire pregnancy. She was literally wasting around this large mass and showed no sign of going into labour well past the due date. My father was about a foot taller than my mother and the baby was enormous. He was getting very concerned about how things were going and took mum to see an obstetrician. The verdict was that she was never going to deliver this baby and that she needed a caesarian section. Dad did not want to worry my mother, who was getting very agitated about the unborn child, and told her that she was going for an anaesthetic and a check-up. A few hours later my elder sister was born. Nothing like uninformed consent.

My sister was a cream coloured version of dad and had his large eyes and round head. Being post-date she was quite shrivelled up and looked as if she had sundown eyes, like a hydrocephalic baby. My mother took one look at her and was shocked. She wondered how such a fine featured girl could produce such a child. In time she unfurled and was, eventually, a bonny baby and very good natured.

Harriet was in heaven as she now had a mini dad, who looked like a Handy. Dad was in heaven because he had a healthy normal child. He was devoted to my sister and would rush back from work to play with her, without even taking a bite to eat or having tea. My sister was ever dad's right hand man and assisted him in all matters. Even the mad dog he had liked her, in spite of never accepting mother. My sister called my father 'Appah' and my mother 'Ammah'. For ease, they then started calling each other the same to avoid confusion. Harriet became Appammah (father's mother), but Iyah was always Iyah to everyone.

This was a wonderful time in their lives, when Ammah savoured motherhood and my sister and the dog cried and barked when dad left for work and glued themselves to the window until he returned. He sometimes worked very long hours, occasionally even for days at a time, but hospital quarters were nearby so he would pop in for meals and the odd afternoon nap. His worst attachment was paediatric neurosurgery, not only for its unsociable hours, but also because he hated operating on children. He dreaded going back to work to find that some of the little fellows who had followed him around had died. He also performed some fairly heroic surgery; kids with subdural haemorrhages (a bleed under the skull) having burr hole surgery in the lift to stop their brains from compressing.

One little boy on the ward was an orphan who was very bright and had a tumour of his skull bone. This was successfully removed and his brain unaffected but now only covered by scalp. Dad had a metal skull cap fashioned for him that fitted over his head to literally protect his brain. All was going well but no one would care for him long term, such was their fear of anything going wrong. Dad really liked the bright little chap and as he could not stay on the wards forever, he came to stay with us.

My mother felt sorry for the lad but was not overjoyed at the responsibility. Sensing her anxiety, Kantheswami used to run up trees and hang off them, whilst she screamed for fear that he would fall and smash his brains on the ground. In today's world no one would trust their simple kindness. They would need police clearance and have to fill out several forms in triplicate. This would all take years whilst the child languished in some institution, precious time lost.

Another person that came to stay was a girl called Nancy. Her family had been Indian Tamils who had worked on the tea estates. She too had been orphaned and was staying with an uncle and was being treated quite badly. There were rumours that she had been the victim of abuse. The poor girl was small and malnourished and Appah and Ammah took her in as well. She did some chores for us and assisted Ammah.

I was their second child and no trouble at all. My mother was disappointed that I was not a boy as, for all the grandchildren Iyah had, there was no Sanders boy. I was born in Jaffna hospital and christened at St James church. My Uncle Rajan (Daniel) attended this event with barely veiled disappointment.

'The good Lord has blessed us with a lovely girl,' the minister declared.

'I wish the good Lord would bestow His blessings in the right proportion,' was my Uncle's cryptic response.

My grandfather wrote, 'a rosebud is born.' I'm not boasting, just quoting what he wrote.

My sister was none too pleased at my arrival and glued herself to Appah's side. To ensure that the attention was not side-tracked she promptly became ill and landed up in hospital dehydrated. The new resident had several failed attempts at getting a drip into her, in order to commence hydration. She started screaming, 'Jesus Papa help me.' The good Lord was clearly listening and Appah finally pushed the young doctor aside and put it in himself. She got better.

I had lots of curly hair and was very chatty with everyone I met. This irritated my sister beyond belief and she found me to be a little show-off. We moved again to Rajagirya in Colombo. Appah had worked hard and impressed, he was promoted to assistant District Medical Officer (DMO) in Colombo. We were moving up in the world.

My first language was Sinhalese, as we lived in a Sinhalese area; later I learned English and finally Tamil. Over the years I have made exceptional progress and now I speak only English.

After two caesarean sections my mother was advised to have no more children. She was not happy on two counts. First, she was aiming for four children and second, there was still no Sanders boy. Her third pregnancy was a nightmare from the beginning. She bled throughout and was confined to bed. She also ballooned in weight. I played a lot with the neighbouring boys and was not really bothered. My sister had confirmed from my father that she could still celebrate her birthday if mother died, so she was sanguine

59

about it all too. She had seen an exquisite porcelain tea set in miniature in the shops. It was hand painted with dainty flowers and Appah decided to get it for her early, just in case.

After two sections the womb is very scarred and difficult to open up a third time. My brother started his life as he meant to go on; causing a lot of trouble. He came out bawling so much that he was called *Chandia* or screamer by the nurses. In the process of delivery my mother's bladder had been inadvertently slashed and no one noticed. She was all sewn up and popped back on the ward.

My sister and I were being looked after by my Aunt Ranee and the baby was brought for viewing by one of the nurses. She had him in a basket bundled up in white sheets and he was crying his head off. I remember thinking, 'I hope this little demon is not coming home with us. Maybe we could just leave him at the hospital, or better still, get rid of him.'

My mother remained on the ward longer than expected because she kept getting infections which did not respond to the limited range of antibiotics available. No small wonder. She then started to rigor. We were so pleased that the tea set had been purchased prematurely. My father was pacing the ward and he and his fellow doctors were wondering what to do next. They then came upon the novel idea of pumping bicarbonate into the bladder. This would alter the PH and make it less favourable to bacteria. It was a eureka moment, though not so pleasant for Ammah as it made her breathless and feel as if she was drowning. She had implicit trust in whatever Appah was doing and in due course improved.

Meanwhile Ranee was struggling at home with *Chandia*. I suppose he must have been missing his parents. Ranee used to shake up his milk bottles so that they looked like cappuccino, so on reflection he probably had gas and colic. Patience was never a virtue with my aunt but she struggled on. She must have been in her late teens at the time and was a decade younger than my mother, so it was kind of her to come and stay and help us out. She was always great fun to be around and was more like one of us than one of the adults.

Everywhere she went she drew wolf whistles and stares. This used to happen even when my sister and I were teenagers and she was middle aged. We were ever so flattered till we realised that the admiration was not for us. We were teenage girls; it just was not fair. She soaked up all the attention.

Appah used to tease Ranee relentlessly. One night she was out on the porch and he was in his study behind her. He switched off the lights and placed a skull on the window and lit its eyes with a torch. On turning around she started shouting and screaming, bringing the entire neighbourhood to our door. No one could understand what the hysteria was about and, before she could formulate the words to explain herself, Dad said, 'Sometimes she screams for nothing!'

Another member of our family was Roger the dog. My father had always owned dogs, but after marrying my mother they were never allowed in the house. That may sound cruel, but it is warm in the East and we had large verandas and land, so many people took this approach. Roger was a cross between a Great Dane and an Alsatian and inherited the worst traits of each. He looked cute enough when he arrived tiny in a cardboard box. Some relative palmed him off on us and his brother went to my Uncle Rajan.

My father exercised him a lot and went to the butcher regularly and got him tripe and other favourites. He grew to gigantic proportions and had a bark that could shake our house. My mother and I shared one thing in common. We truly hated Roger. He was the worst tempered beast you could imagine. When my mother tried to feed him, he would jump at her. When standing, he was nearly Dad's height so this was terrifying. My mother then changed her tactic and used to push his meals out to him with a broom and even then he would lunge at the broom.

The dog loved Appah and did whatever he wanted. Somewhere along the line he decided that he also loved my sister and would allow her to ride him like a horse. He knew my mother and I disliked him and he detested us in equal measure. If he was not tied up, I would avoid going to the garden and it felt like I was imprisoned in my home. I wonder at my father permitting the existence of this monster in our midst but my nephew Sam, who is our animal expert, tells me he probably had no idea what he was getting into. Apparently this type of mix is a 'one man dog.' Dad was the boss, Rosh was tolerated and all else were vermin.

On the plus side he was great for security. The postman, milkman, any man would never dare to venture to our door but instead would drop whatever off by the gate. On one occasion someone really did try to rob us and our treasured pet bit him. Lights went on, and off, and my father was running around the house to get the thief with his old *mamety* (old fish knife). They made a threatening pair, Dad and Roger.

The next day a policeman came to see us but this time not with regard to Dad's work but with a complaint that our dog had bitten someone. Dad laughed his head off and told them the fellow more than deserved it. The policeman looked at him pleadingly and said, 'Look, sir, you know that and I know that, but we can't prove it and we all know about your dog. I suggest that you give the man a few rupees to help his recovery, otherwise I may need to shoot your dog.' I would have definitely chosen to shoot the dog but sadly Appah paid up.

When we went on holiday, usually to Guru Vasa, no one would take the dog so he had to come with us. We had to use a cattle chain to harness him as he would bite through all dog alternatives. When my large, dark father and the dog walked the streets it was like witnessing the parting of the waves; people would scatter. He looked like Mr Rochester and my mother, being not so much plain Jane but more like a dainty doll taken hostage.

The neighbours had a little pup that used to play with Roger, brave thing. One day, the pup bit Roger's ear. Dad was away and infection set in at a terrific rate, as it can in the heat of the tropics. Being bad tempered he allowed no one near him to fix it. When Dad came back it was too late and Roger was gravely ill. The vet was terrified and would not approach him and advised that the dog should be put down. So Dad took the injections of morphine, held him close and gave him a shot.

The next morning Roger was up and barking again. Appah had to go back to the vet and get a double dose and do it all again. The vet was amazed and said that the amount of morphine given could usually kill at least four dogs. It was like the scene in *I am Legend*; he held the dog close as only he could do and injected him. This time Roger really did die. I was delighted, but it was the only time my sister and I saw our father cry.

Life moved on at a busier pace in Colombo and we were now near all our cousins and met up regularly. There were also the trips to Guru Vasa for Christmas when we caught up with our grandparents. Iyah hated leaving home, unlike Appammah, who was a great traveller. He only ventured forth if he had some medical ailment that could not be dealt with in Jaffna. Even then he would stay the minimum period possible. He arrived once to have prostate surgery and stayed with my parents.

One day, my grandfather was walking about the compound of our house when he smelt something atrocious. Round and round the house he went but he could not quite locate the smell. He eventually called my father and, tapping the boot of his car with his stick, demanded that it was opened. It was only then that Appah remembered the decaying specimen in the boot, and took off in haste to his pathology lab in hospital.

The police would also pick up some unusual characters and bring them home for Appah to examine. This happened at all hours and we loved to watch. We had made a small hole from our room to his office which gave us an adequate view. We knew the drill quite well. The person would usually be drunk and since there was no biochemical way of testing this, the doctor would ask his befuddled patient basic questions. If he failed he was taken away and locked up for being 'drunken and disorderly', and if not the next step was hospital for further investigation.

One day the constables brought in a Chinese man. He answered all the questions wrongly and, trying to be helpful, my sister shouted, 'It's Friday, you fool.' My father was unimpressed and the Chinese gentleman, raging when he was taken away to spend a night in jail. As he was marched off, he gave my father a vicious look and said, 'We will get you one day. One day China will rule the world, you wait and see.' Very prophetic words spoken, for today it is the Chinese sun that shines on Sri Lanka.

Appah knew a number of policemen because of his job. Instead of being on the wrong side of the law, as he was a decade before as a medical student, he was now respectable and presumed to be on the right side. He used to speed his cars along the Colombo Road and was invariably stopped. Once they saw who was in the car, the policemen would apologise for making an error. How I wish speed cameras in the UK worked liked that; I would be financially considerably better off.

In the beginning, my father did not want to be a doctor but was co-opted by Harriet. He had dragged his heels through medical school and barely passed. Once he had started working for people in the villages and small hospitals, he loved it and excelled. Now he had made his way to Colombo, step by step. The hitch was that he had been allocated forensic medicine by the government. No choices in the good old days, the country trained you and then they told you what was needed for your country and you simply did it. He disliked forensic medicine because he hated dealing with lawyers and courts. He had an honest, straightforward outlook on things which was not helpful in his job. He also disliked it because it was not curative medicine.

The title of DMO Colombo sounds very grand but it was a poisoned chalice. No DMO lived very long. They generally died soon after getting the job from natural or sometimes unnatural causes. His predecessor had found the whole thing too much and the vacancy was created because he had had a heart attack and passed away. My mother continually worried about how the stress accompanying this post would affect my father.

One of the cases that caused a lot of trouble was brought against a then popular MP. He had assaulted someone and was about to get away scot-free. The only tell-tale sign of his well-crafted fabrications was a lost finger. The evidence given by my father was critical to the case and he was visited by several prominent members of the government and offered bribes, all of which he refused. He came under hideous pressure and would not be intimidated. It was like a scene from the book *To Kill A Mockingbird* when the lawyer Atticus Finch cannot be made to take the side of his white neighbours against an innocent black man. The whole village turns against him but he is stubborn as a mule. His black housekeeper applauding his courage says to his daughter, 'Miss Jean Louise, stand up. Your father's passin.'

Atticus was an unlikely hero and all around us there are these types. Our unsung heroes pass us by daily on the street.

My father then entered the dark days of his life. Every doctor in Ceylon, if he wanted to become anything, had to come to the UK for his post-graduate qualifications. British medicine was thought to be the best in the world and to get these qualifications and come home was a well-trodden path. Appah's own uncle had done this and was the island's most revered cardiologist. Even my father, who was totally devoid of ambition, knew that he had to get out. The government of the day had to authorise these scholarships abroad and he was bypassed on every occasion. People younger than him came and went and he was stuck in a job he hated, with no prospects. If he had just taken a few bribes and done a bit of private practice, we would have all been so much better off.

Nesi decided that the least she could do was to ensure we were dressed in style. She used to get copies of patterns from England and had a seamstress make us very fashionable dresses. My sister and I would be dressed identically, the downside being that I would then grow into her dresses. It felt like I had been wearing the same things for years.

My father used to cut my hair, a fact I was very proud of and shared with the snobbish girls at school. From then on I was pursued with the cries of, 'Your father is a barber.' I had no idea that this was detrimental to me and not an asset.

I disliked school and learning. They were very strict about appearance. Your uniform must be just so with a red buckle, your hair styled in an exact manner and your socks up. I was constantly in trouble about my sloppy appearance and was only saved if I met one of my older cousins, who would procure an extra buckle and quickly mend whatever needed to be mended before the bell went for assembly.

My only asset was my legs. I could run. I could run faster than anyone my age. I could do it without trying. I told my parents this and that they should come and see me at one of the school's sports day. I told them that I would beat everyone and win. They could barely conceal their sniggers. I suppose it seemed unlikely to them because I was quite tubby. My father was late again at work and so both my parents missed my race. I was so angry with him. 'I told you. I told you and you did not believe me!' I cried. 'You ruined it, and why did you tell my friends that you cut my hair?'

Even when life was not running smoothly, my parents enjoyed the day for whatever it brought them. We children were blissfully unaware of their worries and the fact that Ammah was perpetually ill and getting infections, so we carried on our routine. Sundays were best as we usually went to Galle Face Hotel and got ice cream. It always tastes best in the tropics because of the heat and because it is homemade, not commercially produced. It's like chips and brown sauce. You have to have it on a windy, cold day in Edinburgh. It just would not taste the same anywhere else.

After eating as many ice creams as is polite – one is fine, two is just acceptable and three is greedy – we would walk the green. This was a very interesting place with vendors, more food, kite flyers, sailors and lovers. I was easily distracted from following my parents and suddenly found myself without my family and surrounded by a group of men. I had one of my aunt's pretty frocks on and they said I was so cute that they could take me home. I must have been about five and told them that my father was the DMO Colombo and that if they touched me, he would kill them. My parents retrieved me in due course and dad thanked the lads for finding me. Ammah cried, as usual, and smothered my face in nauseating kisses, whilst telling me off simultaneously. I'd just like to say at this point that children are apt to wander and that it is a parental responsibility to ensure that this is not the case.

After ten years of marriage my father had virtually cured himself of spending the day staring at my mother and would occasionally venture to his club. This was an extra special treat for me and my sister, as Ammah was not there to supervise treat consumption and would stay home with the screaming brat. My father would lift us up and perch us on high stools at the bar where we would order goodies to our hearts' content. Meanwhile he would play billiards, have a beer and chat to his friends. One time he briefly vanished and my sister needed the toilet. We were approached by a man who was more than happy to help her. My sister is very trusting in nature and four years my senior. Luckily for her, my brother and I have more of my mother's intuition on these matters.

'No uncle (everyone is referred to as uncle or aunty in Ceylon), we will wait for our father', I said firmly, whilst she was trying to wriggle out of her seat and would have haplessly wondered off with this perv (one of my daughter's favourite words).

Later on Sunday evenings we gathered at some relative's house. The adults tended to sit separately and my Dad's voice could always be heard above all others, usually disagreeing with my Manie Marmic on some juicy topic; either a relative that annoyed him or the government. She was ever diplomatic, which made him madder. My Uncle Kanagarajah was more often on my Dad's side than his wife's but if he wasn't, the noise got even louder as he was a great debater. My mother would laugh too loudly, concealing the fact that she felt ill, had soaked her clothes and needed to change urgently. The cousins would practise a dance or song to show off to the adults. I would invariably embarrass myself by eating too much and needing a tummy rub with tiger balm and then we would all go home to start a new week.

At the next election the government changed and Appah got a letter to say that his scholarship had been approved for the UK. He was on his way. When he was walking the street he bumped into a man, who insisted on reading his hand. People do that sort of stuff in the East and Dad, feeling buoyant, gave him a few coins and humoured him.

'You will leave your country and it will never be the same', he told him. 'You will have success but you will never live here again.' My father laughed and rushed home to tell my mother the good news about his scholarship.

66

Ammah wanted Appah to go to Britain. She could see that if he stayed without further postgraduate qualifications he would constantly be bypassed for promotion and that he would eventually become very frustrated. She also carried a secret guilt that, had he married the *right* sort of girl, all sorts of doors would have opened to him and that he would have gone and come back by now. Instead he picked her and was content to sit around holding her hand and confirming what everyone had suspected, that 'Sanders was a loser'.

The previous government allowed spouses to go on scholarship and funded them, but the new government did not. Appah was very concerned about leaving Ammah. He knew my mother was ill, though all the doctors reassured him that it was nothing serious. Doctors' wives are after all notorious somatisers; what do you expect when a man works all hours? You have to do something to get a bit of attention.

He had a sneaky suspicion that the bladder had been nicked and that my mother had a fistula. All the symptoms fitted: repeated infections, uncontrolled flooding and monthly blood in the urine. After three caesarean sections, it would take a brave man to open up the doctor's wife and fix her. He knew of a world expert in Liverpool who could do it and he wanted my mother to go with him to Britain.

There were, as always, a few small problems. They had no free flow of cash for this and they had three children under ten. Banks then did not lend money, perhaps that was wise on reflection, given our current circumstances. The Ceylonese rupee was like Monopoly money when pitched against the British pound and the government only allowed you to take out a limited quantity – the equivalent of £3 was the exact sum. I used to think this was quite mean but now I begin to see the light.

My father asked my bewildered mother to pack her bags, though he had no evidence to fuel his determination that he was not leaving without her. 'Get ready and we will see how it goes', was what he told her. See how it goes? How do you get a vast quantity of money, when you have none? He was going to another continent, not on the yaldevi train to Jaffna. What about the children, had anyone noticed they were quite small? One child was overly trusting and would wander off with anyone, one was pining and the other screamed so much you wanted to put a pillow over his face. Who was going to be supernanny? My mother being my mother, instead of talking sense to him, packed her bags and laughed.

This was how my parents lived their lives. All right, it was not looking good, but be of good cheer, do what you can and live in hope. Appah and Ammah had a lot of good friends. They nurtured their relationships in a way that others nurtured their ambition and position. Ceylon Tamils are a particularly hard-nosed driven lot and are not called the 'Jews of the East' for nothing. One of Dad's friends, a Dr Pasupathyrajah, posted him two tickets to England. What a pal! What if he had not?

My parents looked at boarding Roshini and me at Ladies' College. Can you imagine? It was bad enough being at school all day when you were not keen to learn. Would I be woken in the middle of the night and asked to tidy my hair? Would my curly locks be cut off for not sitting straight, like Jane Eyre's friend? The brat saved us because he was two years old and my parents thought him too young to board. Wasn't that really thoughtful? Personally I think it would have altered his personality for the better, all that screaming was clearly a lack of discipline.

Supernanny then appeared in the form of an octogenarian. My grandfather came to save us from our parents' cunning plan. Things were then moving swiftly and before you knew it all relatives were assembled in Kattunayaka airport and crying. In fact the airport was full of crying people because Ceylonese do not believe in 'the stiff upper lip' and cry when you leave and cry when you arrive. There were bags floating about with last minute things being poked into them to breaking point. My father was getting angry and people were pushing and shoving, a general feeling of chaos ensued.

My father then took my sister aside and told her; didn't she know she was his right hand man? She was to look after the two little ones and not give Iyah and Appammah any trouble. She was to be a good girl and work hard. He would come back for her soon. Her goggly eyes were wide and she was nodding at his every word. I wanted to say, 'I look after *her*, you know. She hasn't got a clue and now Miss Bossy-Boots is going to be even worse. Thanks for that.' My mother was doing the rounds, doing that crying, kissing thing, that made me sick. This was all a ploy to make us feel sorry for them, when *we* were being dumped and *they* were going on holiday. I knew what it was. It was what people do years after they get married, a second honeymoon. I wished they would just go and leave me alone.

I remember standing on the balcony at the airport. My face is pressed against the bars and I am looking at the plane. The brat is screaming and my sister is gulping. The plane is making a big noise. It is going way, way up, way up in the sky. Did they really mean it? How can they leave me here?! I am not going to cry. They can go on their stinky holiday.

My grandfather is holding my hand. He tells me everything is going to be just fine. We are going to Guru Vasa, we are going to have a good time and then my parents will be back.

'When?' I ask.

'Soon,' he smiles.

'A few days?', I say and he elusively smiles again, but the days turned into weeks and the weeks turned into months and the months turned to years and they never came back for me.

So you see, love is not a many splendored thing. It abandons you and lets you down. When you see it coming, walk away, or sooner or later you will get hurt.

CHAPTER 8

# GURU VASA

I met my cousin in London recently. Whilst we were having dinner at a Sri Lankan restaurant, a West Indian came in with his girlfriend and started talking using occasional Tamil words. I thought it quite strange, until my cousin informed me that he was Tamil.

'Why is he acting as if he was West Indian?' I say naively (you can tell I come from Scotland).

'Because it's a cool thing to be.'

How sad. Isn't it cool to be yourself? Nothing against West Indians or any other race but we all have something to be proud of. It's like in *Who Do You Think You Are?* Every family has its hero and villains, its prince and pauper.

My cousin orders lump rice for me. If you have one last meal on earth this is it. It is frequently served at Ceylonese weddings and feasts. It is labour intensive to prepare but when the guests have arrived you simply heat in the oven and hand out, which leaves you free to be a social butterfly.

First you get a banana leaf (tin foil if you are in the UK). Place pre-cooked sambar rice in the middle. This is the king of rice, not basmati as the adverts lead you to believe. The grains are like little pearls and maintain their shape for even the worst cook and never go mushy. In one corner you add blow-your-head-off mutton curry, in another deep fried aubergine curry, next a fish cutlet and/or a boiled egg and finally *seeni sambol*. My mother used to make her own with deep fried tiny *maldive* fish and onions, but it takes forever and can be found ready-made in any Sri Lankan shop in London. In case your palate now explodes with the chilli, you pour lots of coconut milk on top, wrap it up and you're done.

If you are a vegetarian like some of my family, pray to God that in the next life you will be a meat-eater. You really have missed out.

My cousin orders a Kingfisher beer, which is definitely Indian and cheating but Sri Lankan alcoholic drinks are disgusting, so I let him off. Since he has recently passed a significant birthday I ask him,

'When you look back, what has been the best part of your life so far?'

'That's easy', he says. 'The Guru Vasa days.'

After my parents left us to embark upon their second honeymoon, my grandparents took us back to Guru Vasa, as promised. Up until then it had been our holiday home, but now it was the real thing. We were in Colombo so had to board the famous Colombo to Jaffna train to get to Nallur.

Now this was an adventure. The stations in the east are noisy places full of coolies rushing about with bags and vendors and people crying like in the airport. The trains were still the old British ones and beautifully crafted. You could get a private carriage for your family which consisted of beds, a small lounge area and en-suite. The internal furnishings were exquisitely designed from solid wood and brass, proudly embossed with British manufacturing names. If you were really well-off, you could even have a suite of inter-connecting carriages.

We passed station upon station. In the south it was so lush and green. The earth burst forth in its exuberance and ever present there was that tropical, hot, damp feeling. The train rushed past village after village; paddy fields, coconut plantations, banana groves; men in sarongs ploughing their fields, ladies carrying baskets of produce to sell, children in white uniform rushing to school. Ha ha! No school for us today.

So much wildlife flashed before my eyes. Then parts of the island still had jungle, untouched by man and the train rushed through it. Monkeys, elephants, wildcats and exotic birds put on a display for our benefit. My brother loved the monkeys; after all he had much in common with them.

As you went north the land was less yielding. There was a drier heat and the ground was red. Here the tall, slender, palmyra tree was king, unlike in the

72

south where there were coconut trees in abundance. It was a harsher land.

Every so often a smooth, white dagoba would rise above the earth. There was something calm and simplistic about them. When you go north these changed to the noisy colourful temples of the Hindus. Bells ring, people chant.

I listened out for the cries of the vendors at each station.

*'Vaddai vaddai vaddai!'* We frequently bought something small, the anticipation was enormous and the journey passed quickly.

On arrival Vincent was there with his car. When Iyah had a car, Vincent was his driver. Now Vincent had his own car but would regularly work for us when we needed him. Vincent looked like a film star and was obliging and reliable too, so he got plenty of work to keep him going. He had known us all for years and was part of the family.

Nancy came with us to Guru Vasa to help my grandmother look after us. She clearly thought Vincent looked like a film star too. Unlucky for her that he already had a wife appropriately named Lovely.

My grandparents were not happy to have Kanthaswami to come and stay. The responsibility was simply too much for them. He went back to his village to live with a distant relative. Appah had given him some money but we heard that when the money ran out, he was not so well treated. I hate to think what became of him.

We made our way to Navallar road and Guru Vasa was situated just by the Katcheri junction. The house had large double gates to permit the cars to be driven in and a single gate for people on foot. A partition ran between the two and started at calf level up, so that you could see people's feet go by but not the rest of them. The front compound had several mango trees but my grandparents pride and joy was the cycus tree.

Cycus trees are not native to Ceylon but can be found in Africa, Portugal or the Middle East. They have a thick ringed base and relatively less foliage than the coconut tree or palmyra. They look bottom-heavy but this makes them very stable and they are also very, very slow growing like the yew tree in Britian.

Our cycus tree was thought to be several hundred years old. It was certainly there when Guru Nagar, our original ancestor, bought the land. C.C. Handy built the house but left the tree untouched. My father noted a large number of these trees in Madeira when he travelled there and wondered if a Portuguese sailor had accidentally dropped this seed four hundred years before.

All the cousins referred to Guru Vasa as their house but it was technically my aunt's. She had got it as dowry but stayed somewhere else and at this point my grandparents had only 'life interest'. The house had passed from C.C. Handy, to Harriet and then to my aunt Chandra.

This meant that my grandparents could stay there as long as they lived but it was no longer theirs. This led to some interesting situations. Things needed fixing but my grandfather was cautious to do this, as it was no longer his property. The house had seen better days and was definitely in need of some renovation but he left that to my aunt and Ratnarajah uncle to deal with.

The great thing about ageing is that my grandparents had failing vision, so they did not seem to notice the paint peeling off the walls, cracked steps and faulty shutters. For our part we couldn't care less. People in the East do not spend a lot of time in their homes. The veranda is the place to be. If you live in a cold climate and the reverse is true, you become quite involved with the colours of your walls, soft furnishings and accessories.

Guru Vasa had a few steps leading up to the veranda and on these my grandmother had large pots and planted vibrant athuriums and cannas of all colours. These took some looking after in the harsh dry Jaffna heat. Iyah's pride and joy were his pink climbing roses which clambered over the walls. I swear he counted each flower, for if you dared pick one he always knew.

The building was U shaped. On the front veranda to the left we have Iyah's easy chair, or planters chair. Sit on that and you will get a stare that withers you. Beyond that is a hall where you can play all day and where your parents' things will be stored in old tea chests. To the left, a table and more chairs where you can sit. A good place for playing cards, eating monkey nuts and watching legs go by.

Enormous double doors open and Italian tiles of intricate design usher you into the dark cool lounge. There are settees under the shuttered windows. These double up as beds for when the cousins come. In the corner, at the back, Iyah's radio and more chairs. Don't touch the radio either. On the right there is an old piano where my grandmother plays impassionedly and is young again.

Bedrooms flank each side of the lounge. Rosh and I will sleep in the one on the left. Iyah, Appammah and the brat will be in the one on the right. I love this arrangement; I can get a full night's sleep for the first time in years, as the brat used to be in a cot with us. I am sure my grandmother will cope fine. Old people don't sleep anyway. Beyond Iyah and Appammah's room is his office.

Don't even think about going there. The half hall room next to this is where Appammah hides her imported food stuff and she thinks we and the servants do not know.

Behind the lounge is the dining room and a half kitchen, (I'll come back to that), as well as a back veranda to the left and another bedroom on the right.

At the back, on the right wing we have a large toilet and on the left wing the servants' rooms and another large kitchen. Why two kitchens you may ask? Is one for cooking and the other for showing off? The main kitchen was indeed at the back but my grandmother was an excellent cook and hostess and some things she liked to prepare for herself. There were also eats like *hoppers* (a type of pancake) that had to be served instantly and the transit time from the proper kitchen to table was, in my grandmother's opinion, too long.

In the lands at the back the goats and chickens lived. Iyah had a goat called Nita for years and she had two kids Blackie and Brownie, who were our pets. You could eat from the banana, paw paw or mango tree. Appammah may ask for assistance to harvest drumstick or limes for dinner if the servants were too busy. We never voluntarily consumed any of these.

Right at the back was the outside toilet. You had to be pretty desperate to use it and it was a relic from the olden days before flushing toilets were invented. For this reason alone I am delighted that I was born in the twentieth century.

We rapidly settled into a routine. My sister, Miss Bossy and I had to go to school and she took it upon herself to supervise my toileting and dressing. She packed my school bags, checked my homework and was compelled to tell me what to do at every twist and turn. Appammah used to wage war on my unruly locks and rub my scalp vigorously with coconut oil. This is used in Ceylon in small quantities and is claimed to nourish the scalp and works a bit like conditioner. My grandmother could not see very well and so I was drowned in the stuff and went to school looking as if I had crawled out of the deep fat fryer. She would ensure that we had a massive breakfast, a bit like the dinners we have today, with rice and curry and fish. The brain could not function without sugar she said, but with my results it was clearly making no difference.

Vincent came then for us in his car, which we shared with other children and our beautiful dance teacher, who was nearly as pretty as Ammah. If the car was crowded she would let me sit on her lap and was always very kind to me. I am sure I put big oily stains on her exquisite saris but she did not seem to mind. She had long, slender limbs as dancers do and was very poised.

Sometimes Iyah would let me pluck one of his pink roses and I would always give them to her.

School at Chundukkuli was just as hateful as Colombo with the added pressure that I now had to do more in Tamil, my third language. Keen not to blot my perfect record of being a dunce and disinterested, I started as I meant to go on, paying no attention to lessons at all.

My sister was being Miss Perfect and excelled in all things. My one consolation was that I could run faster than her, even though she was four years older than me. My grandparents came to see all my races and my grandfather would buy me two ice creams for winning. He did not seem to mind that I was doing badly at school and was very tolerant of my shortcomings.

Meanwhile the brat was quite quiet at home. He did not scream so much anymore but he did not talk much either and looked sickly and emaciated. He was not eating all the wonderful things Appammah made. I used to feel a bit sorry for him and sometimes even tried to play games with him, but if he lost he started the screaming again and I would lose patience.

My brother's role model was a man called 'Crack John'. He probably had a mental illness and was a great collector of goods. He tied these precious items to a string and then around his waist and walked the Navallar road. The more items that he had, the happier he was. He was a very friendly man and talked to all as he passed. My brother strove to emulate him and walked round and round Guru Vasa with his precious discoveries tied around his waist, making quite a clatter. I marvel at my grandparents' patience tolerating this unusual behaviour. I think they thought we were a bit disturbed and were very gentle with me and my brother.

For Appammah, 'Roshy' my sister, could do no wrong and so to compensate Iyah was quite harsh on her. She probably asked for it. He was never unkind to me. This was a repetition of the situation with Appah all over again. Ever attention-seeking in her behaviour she developed abdominal pain and eventually even my grandparents had to give in and take her to hospital. The doctors claimed she nearly burst her appendix and she was in hospital for over a week. I visited her dutifully every day. She was only allowed a simple diet and was encouraged to consume a lot of ice cream and jelly. She was feeling too sickly to eat it, so my main reason for visiting was to help her out. The jelly was bright red and flavoured like the strawberries they have in Britain.

Trips to Mathagal were another culinary treat as we 'orphans' were spoilt by our mother's family. My aunt Nesi came for us one day and told us that Appu (mum's dad) was dying again, so we needed to see him one last time. He had had several strokes by now and was quite muddled and asking for my mother. My aunt decided to get Roshy to feed him and pretend to be Ammah. I could not believe that he fell for it and rested back content. She looked nothing like my mother and they really should have asked me. Anyone will tell you that my sister is the spitting image of dad. Soon after this event Appu passed away peacefully and the 'honeymooners' received a telegram to say so, and that their daughter had been in hospital too but was better. They say my mother cried a lot.

My aunt Ranee's visits were the ones I looked forward to most. She was such fun to be with. My grandparents would give her vast instruction on what we were allowed and not allowed to do, being elderly and over cautious, as we were not their children. She would smile sweetly and as soon as we turned the corner all restrictions were lifted. Listening to the voice of authority would be a first for my aunt. Even when we lived in Colombo we used to spy on her secret rendezvous with her boyfriend. They were openly affectionate to each other and we would scurry after them giggling and chanting our nonsensical rhymes in their wake.

*Thanaballs has gone to sea,*
*Silver buckles on his knee*
*He'll come back and marry me*
*Thanapalasingam.*

They did get married after this and lived in Mathagal too, but my aunt never took us there. We headed for the movies and saw adult films where people nearly kissed! The best of these was 'Kathirupane unakka;' 'I will wait for you.' She also allowed three or even four treats at a time, *Vimto, bulto, thummbu muttas* (a bit like candy floss) and anything else we wanted.

We would weave our way through forbidden streets and stores bursting with produce, the bangle shop, the material store and best of all a toy shop. We also loved to go to the temples to hear the chanting and smell the incense and stare at the colourful Gods. We returned to Guru Vasa late and were sworn to secrecy.

Meanwhile, back at home, Nancy seemed to be sneaking around with some chap too. Appammah kept losing things and worrying about her failing memory. Someone had apparently prised opened our parents' tea chests in the half hall room, which bothered her. We kept quiet for this bit, as we knew it was us.

My parents treated Nancy like part of the family but my grandparents were of a different generation. They did not mistreat her but the boundaries were clearer. She had her own bit of the house, which I think made her lonely. The kitchens were also distant to the main body of the house and she did not come with us when we went to the town or to the movies as before.

One day we woke to find that she had run away, taking quite a few of our possessions and Appammah's things too. At least Appammah could now be relieved that she was not losing things and becoming demented as she feared.

You really couldn't blame Nancy. A friend of a friend saw her on a bus many years later. Apparently she was happily married with children; I'd like to hope so.

We let Nancy take the blame for opening the tea chests. She was gone now, so what did it matter? My parents had stored their things in them and most importantly their letters to each other. We had a great laugh at these and showed them to our friends and cousins who enjoyed them too.

The biggest party was when our cousins came at Christmas. Appammah would go into overdrive and produce her wonderful rich cake. I cannot talk about the recipe, as it is a family secret. For days, the house smelled of spices, dried fruit and cinnamon; we have the best in the world in Ceylon. She would also make *laddu*, *chippie* and *thodus*, intricate sweets for our many visitors.

Every visitor at Christmas got a small gift and so the rich cake was laboriously wrapped each year with different colourful, delicate, papers and handed over reluctantly by us children.

Our Kanagarajah cousins would always arrive with a lot of books. The three girls were like the Brontë sisters, very learned and articulate. Many of the Kanagarajahs wore glasses, which I thought was another good reason not to spend too much time reading. They were our great story tellers.

My Ratnarajah cousins were the musicians and also were privy to all family events, births, deaths, marriages and the latest movies, which they would relate with precision and detail.

The boys from each family would argue at length about cricket matches and sporting activities. Who was best at batting, who was the fastest runner?

When my uncle Rajan was in Sri Lanka things were even noisier. He, Kanagarajah Uncle, my father and his cousin Mano were like the 'Brat Pack'. They loved being together and would debate till the early hours and even be quite rude to each other with shouts of:

'That bugger is talking rubbish.' (Everyone is a bugger in Ceylon if you do not like him, or he annoys you. My father knew a lot of buggers).

'What nonsense *Chinacca*', would reverberate around the house.

In the background Iyah would be in a rage with the *dobbie* for mixing up all our clothes with someone else's. Appammah could be overheard in vast negotiation with the vendors, particularly as supplies had to be multiplied for her hungry brood.

In its heyday, the dining room would easily seat thirty people, with Iyah at its helm. Appammah was in her element, feeding her vocal offspring whilst contributing to the arguments with the sharpest observations of all. The adults sat at the top of the table and the children at the bottom. We liked it this way, so that we could quietly dispense with any vegetable dishes we did not like.

The most artistic cousin handmade many of the decorations for the Christmas tree, which was only put up on Christmas Eve. The cousins loved to sleep on the veranda all together and would chat till the small hours under the starlight. Christmas morn invariably involved a groggy start to the day, as we kept each other up all night with our chatter. The alarm went off at a gruelling 6 a.m. and woe betide anyone late for church. It was a military campaign to toilet and feed the lot and get everyone out in time. Cars would come for us, but my grandfather would walk as always.

The presents were simple affairs – a book, colour pencils, tiddlywinks. We were delighted with them and knew no better. Food was dispatched to poorer homes and offerings for the poor in church extra generous.

Because of this even now I never buy the children large gifts at Christmas on principle; 'Birthdays are different, for they are about you', is what I tell them. They seem to accept this line or maybe they go to school and tell their friends that they have the stingiest parents on the planet!

Back in London my cousin asks me if I will have dessert. I should know better but I order a *vatillupum*. It's not great; I should have gone for the Indian kulfi that they are trying to palm off as Sri Lankan.

My pseudo-West Indian friend is making quite a racket and force feeding his girlfriend something. I have the urge to go over and smack him on the head. It's a middle-aged mother impulse, when I see someone behaving inappropriately. My cousin is more tolerant and smiles.

'When did you last see Iyah?' I ask.

'During the 1977 elections. All hell had broken loose and the government imposed a curfew. We were trapped in Guru Vasa for a month. Finally Iyah managed to get a car for us late one night, to assist in our escape. We had got air tickets to the Seychelles and Zambia – anywhere but Ceylon. We were packed and waiting on the veranda and lights were flashing. It was terrifying. Tanks were travelling down the Navallar Road. Once they had passed we made our way quietly. Our car crossed the Katcheri junction and we strained for our last look at Guru Vasa. Iyah was standing defiantly in the middle of the Navallar Road, waving us all goodbye.'

What he did not say is that if you disobeyed the curfew you could be shot.

CHAPTER 9

# DESCENT
# TO CHAOS

Appah and Ammah arrived in London on a bleak October morning. Mummy had on one of her delicate crépe georgette saris, sandals and no coat. I suppose it was best to get used to the sensation of freezing as soon as possible.

One of their friends, Donald Rajapaksa, met them and reorganised their wardrobes, and educated them with a rough guide on how to survive.

They then made their way to Glasgow, or so they thought. They found the Glaswegian accents hard to decipher, like most Brits do, never mind foreigners, and so boarded the wrong bus. The bus took them to Port Glasgow several miles away. The place was unappealing and they were a bit shocked, but once they got to Glasgow, having realised their error, they felt a little better.

Getting accommodation was a major headache. As soon as they found something vaguely acceptable, at the right price and started walking up the path with their suitcases full of anticipation, the *No Blacks* signs went up. It took them a while to realise that this meant them. They were brown, not black for a start. On the plus side, they had no children, no pets and were not Catholic.

Finally they found a bedsit with shared toilet and no bath. The shared toilet was bad enough and my mother had to supress waves of nausea and revulsion every time she entered it but the public bath was a real 'wee challenge'.

The public bath is hard to imagine, in our en-suite days of today. Here you would queue up with the city's underworld, your towel and toiletries in hand. It was a bit like camping, but with a more interesting clientele. You were then supplied with cleaning agents and it was hoped that after a brief spell in the bath, you would give it a little clean and then be off. Appah and Ammah quickly got quite intimate with the drunks and prostitutes of Glasgow. They were friendly people with a tale to tell, but you had to be sure you had locked your door, or you would come out of your bath with nothing but your birthday suit.

Appah went on his attachment to the forensic unit each day and worked with Professor Forbes, a giant in this field in his time. Ammah stayed behind in their 'flat' and cried. Professor Forbes gave Dad a Christmas card and it had a choir boy trying to sing, but completely distracted by the mouse (i.e. mum) in his back pocket, diverting his attention.

My parents moved around a lot as my father gained experience in different units. Dad had a spell with Professor Keith Simpson described as the UK's finest forensic pathologist in the famous Guy's Hospital, London. Later he moved again to Edinburgh.

With their limited scholarship finances, Dad walked everywhere rather than taking the bus and this meant he shed all those pounds of lard my mother had put on him since marriage. He also took a packed lunch which was lovingly prepared and consisted of two slices of bread with something in the middle. The something, fifty per cent of the time, was egg and the other fifty per cent of the time was Spam, a sort of reconstituted meat that looked much like what we used to feed Roger the dog.

One day he came home early and blasted my mother for sitting in the cold. I am sure she was sensibly trying to acclimatise herself but she claimed that she only fed the heater coins half an hour before he came home.

They were frugal at every twist and turn but the scholarship money was just not enough. My father was studying and shadowing which meant he could not work, as the scholarship finances were barely enough for one and impossible for two. They were very short on funds.

My mother has made an art form all her life of appearing more lightweight than she is, and at this point she braced herself, ditched the sari, cross-stitching and tears and went to work as a nurse.

She had no idea what she had let herself in for and was dismayed at the tasks British nurses were expected to carry out routinely. For example nurses in

Ceylon rarely attended to personal care, as this was carried out by attendants. Angels come to us at times of darkness and this angel was called Ina McKelvie. As the name suggests, she was a buxom motherly sort. Though she could not quite understand my mother's problems, she gaily took over many of the more unpleasant duties expected, leaving mum to do the dispensing of medicines, food, hand holding and comforting patients, which she was good at.

Everything was a challenge to my parents – the damp, cold, sunless climate, the lack of their type of food, the accommodation, the lack of money, but most of all, the lack of friends and family.

It was hard and expensive to make phone calls, there was no texting, email, Skype, webcams or the range of options we have today. If there was an emergency, telegrams were sent and otherwise letters went weekly. Generally I couldn't be bothered writing to them but my grandparents were most diligent in doing so, and encouraged us to do likewise. My sister sent them an audio tape of herself singing 'I'm Nobody's Child', which I thought most appropriate.

Spices were not readily available in Glasgow, though there were Asian food stuffs in London. My parents had to adapt to the indigenous vegetables and the preparation of them, as favourites like aubergines and ladies fingers were nowhere to be found. Leeks were in ample supply, so the revolting mallum made a frequent appearance and they started eating mushrooms, which they never ate in Ceylon, as there they were viewed with suspicion as some sort of poisonous fungus.

As meat eaters, they were better off than some of the Indian vegetarians they met. Even Hindus in Ceylon ate meat but many, including Buddhists and Christians, give this up on a Friday. This meant that they were free to enjoy the joys of Spam six days a week if they wanted to. On special days they got chicken, which was the most expensive meat at home but the cheapest in Britain, which they could not understand. Of course we are now fully informed on why, and those of us who can afford to go 'free range', do.

Dad, in view of his size was not exposed to too much overt racism but would occasionally hear, 'Go home you Paki.'

'I come from Ceylon, not Pakistan, which is an entirely different country and have no worries, I am planning to do just that', he would reply. After a while he knew better and stopped reacting.

My brother recently criticised me for asking the children if they would like 'a Chinky'. He is very P.C. these days, but bearing in mind the husband is 'the Guju (Gujarati)' and the children are 'the mongrels', I can safely say that I am equally racist to all.

Christmas was the worst time of all, as it is for many people if life is not at its best. What was good was that the whole nation celebrated whether they believed or not. Trees and lights and decorations were everywhere and they were a lot more effective in the darkness. Many kindly British people would take foreign students home for Christmas in an effort to make them feel welcome. My parents would gather a few friends, each making a dish and do what they could. These were usually foreigners from all over the world in a similar position.

My father would play jolly Christmas songs on his tape deck but invariably end with 'Country Roads, Take Me Home' by Olivia Newton John and become melancholy. My mother, ever the survivor, would switch it off and smile with gritted teeth.

My mother continued to be the main wage earner for many years and every penny that could be saved was. Some money went to my grandparents for our upkeep and some went on presents for us. There would always be someone who knew someone going back to Ceylon and these would be dutifully delivered to us.

I had told my father before he left that I wanted a 'walkie talkie doll' and one day a friend of theirs did indeed come down the path to Guru Vasa with this life sized dolly in hand. I showed it off to all the girls at school. It was only slightly smaller than me, battery operated and walked and talked. Who was an orphan now? My parents were in England and very well off. Had they not read Dick Whittington? England was the place to be. They were coming for me very, very soon and anyone who had been mean to me would be sorry.

Before they achieved that, there were a few hurdles, like the forensic exams. He who detested studying braced himself and with the knowledge that the longer he took, the longer he would be away from home as a spur to his intent, passed all his forensic qualifications.

The diet of eggs and Spam, as well as the bitter cold weather took its toll and he then caught pneumonia. He was reluctant to go to hospital and leave mum by herself, so he was nursed at home. Their modest rental accommodation was devoid of central heating, the ice was literally on the windows and hair dryers were used on the water pipes to get them flowing again. He had a fabulous immune system and so improved.

The next thing to sort out was my mother's health. Dad made contact with a Liverpool specialist. He was the innovator of a revolutionary technique to visualise the bladder. Dye would be passed up into the bladder and X-rays taken, so problems not visualised on plain film would be revealed. This fantastic, non-invasive procedure told Dad what he already suspected; that my mother's bladder wall and womb were fused together. The surgery would take half a day and involved removing the womb and refashioning the bladder. The patient would need to be catheterised for a month to allow the 'new' bladder to heal before it could work again. A month's stay in hospital would also be required to be cautious and ensure no infection set in.

Whilst they were thinking about how best they should deal with all of this, they started purchasing a few things. A Grundig radio, a Singer sewing machine, a Sony record player. Each item was selected with great care as thought was given to whether it would work in Ceylon and whether we could get batteries and spare parts.

On one of these purchasing expeditions to Princes Street my father passed a man who looked decidedly Ceylonese and a bit lost. He stopped to help him and discovered that he had been a friend of his younger brother, Balan and an ex-student of his father. He invited him for dinner, hopefully not a feast of fried egg. The euphoria of this meeting lasted for days; they must have been as two zebras in a pony field. They remained firm friends for life.

Today the world is a melting pot but still we can occasionally be stopped by a brown face and asked, 'Where are you from?' to which my children respond in disgust 'Scotland' i.e. whatever we are, we are not one of you. They do not understand the desperation of the person, usually a new migrant, asking the question.

News was seeping out about Sri Lanka that things were not so good. Bombs, curfews, civil unrest, communist movements threatening to take over, corruption and heavy handed government reprisals. Dad could not have cared less. He had heard it all before and it never came to anything. He was soon coming home to us and to keep his promise to his parents, that he would care for them in their old age. He used to tell Harriet, 'Don't worry Ammah, I will come back and look after you.' I presume he meant Iyah too.

His Sinhalese friends told him, 'Sandy, you are crazy. Everyone who is anyone is getting out. What man, you are the only fellow trying to get back in.'

For Dad it was a bit like the Scottish/English thing. One group in the north and the other in the south, each claiming superiority for different reasons but in the end they were the same. They were as quarrelsome siblings who had to accept that common blood ran in their veins and for better or worse had to live with each other.

Then they received a telegram from home to say that Iyah had suffered a heart attack and that the children were on their way to Paris in a few days. They somehow made contact with my uncle Daniel, who was in Colombo and going back to the States via France. Over the phone we heard,

'What the hell *Annan*? You are a well-travelled man. France and Britain are separate countries, how am I going to get over there?'

Clearly our father was delighted at the prospect of seeing us. What is nothing now was a mammoth task in the seventies – visas, cash and tickets. They used up all their meagre savings and their friends came to the rescue again. Plans for going home had to be put on hold for gay Paris was calling.

So, such was the hand of fate. My grandfather was exceptionally fit and never ill. If he had kept just so, we would have carried on staying with him in Guru Vasa. My parents would have returned to Sri Lanka the following year. My father loved his country and would have been one of the last to leave, I am sure.

He would have become one of the island's leading forensic specialists and been repeatedly put in challenging situations, especially after civil war broke out. Being a man who would not bend the truth for anyone, I shudder to imagine what would have become of him.

Being able to work and live in Britain saved my father.

*The parents make their way to
Paris as the 'honeymoon' is over.*

*Rajan with us in 1972.*

*The handover in Paris.*

*Ammah and us in Edinburgh 1972. We were miserable!*

*Ammah and friends Margaret and Jane on one of their many coffee mornings.*

*David and his toy robot at Christmas. He had not yet realised that I had broken it.*

*Dr S.C. Sanders Consultant Physician.*

# A Physician's Prayer

Dear Lord, Thou Great Physician,
I kneel before thee. ~~Since~~
Since every good and perfect gift
must come from thee,

## I PRAY :

Give Skill to my hand, clear
vision to my mind, kindness
and sympathy to my heart.
Give me singleness of purpose, strength
to lift at least a part of the burden
of my suffering fellowmen and a true
realization of the privilege that is mine.
Take from my heart all guile and
worldliness that with the simple faith
of a child. I may rely on thee.

1984                    Amen.

*Copy of 'A Physician's Prayer', handwritten by dad.*

*Roshini and Dharshan's wedding, 1988.*

## East central Illinois deaths

### UI dean of social work dead at 61

Funeral services for Daniel S. Sanders, dean of the University of Illinois School of Social Work, will be at 1 p.m. Tuesday at the Wesley Foundation, Urbana, the Rev. Robert McNamara officiating.

Burial will be in Mount Hope Cemetery, Urbana.

Visitation will be from 7 to 8 p.m. today at Renner-Wikoff Chapel, Urbana. Mr. Sanders, 61, of 614 W. Florida Ave., U, died Saturday (Oct. 14, 1989) in San Francisco while attending a National Association of Social Work symposium. He died in his hotel room of an apparent heart attack.

**SANDERS**

Mr. Sanders had been a member of the UI faculty since Jan. 1, 1987.

UI Chancellor Morton W. Weir called Mr. Sanders' death "a tragic loss to the university and the social work profession.

"Dan has brought the school along very nicely during his deanship. His leadership will be missed," Weir said. "Besides his qualities of leadership and scholarship, Dan was a wonderful human being, and that's the quality I will miss the most."

Mr. Sanders was born Sept. 18, 1928, in Jaffna, Sri Lanka. His wife, Christobel, survives.

Also surviving are his mother, Harriet Sanders of Australia; two brothers, Dr. S.C. Sanders of Great Britain and H.B. Sanders of Australia; and two sisters, Pearl Kanagarajah and Rhea Ratnarajah, both of Australia.

Mr. Sanders attended Jaffna College in Jaffna, Sri Lanka. He received a bachelor's degree from the University of Ceylon in 1953.

He earned a diploma in social welfare at the University of Wales in 1958 and a master's degree and a doctorate in 1967 and 1971, respectively, at the University of Minnesota.

While in Sri Lanka, Mr. Sanders was associate director of the Ceylon Institute of Social Work; chairman and founder of the Coordinating Council of Community Development Projects; and executive director of the Institute of Social Study.

Mr. Sanders came to the UI from the University of Hawaii, where he had served as dean and professor of social work and director of international programs.

He was committed to furthering peace and fostering community development in Third World counties.

Mr. Sanders had served as president of the Inter-University Consortium of International Social Development since 1981-In 1988, as president of the organization, he accepted the Messenger of Peace award from the United Nations.

He served on the board of directors of the International Association of Schools of Social Work and was a member of the U.S. Committee of International Conference on Social Welfare.

Memorials may be made to St. Andrew's Lutheran Church, Champaign, and the School of Social Work.

*David whispers sweet nothings into Iman's ear with no idea that they are being watched.*

*My wedding with Scottish, Indian and Sri Lankan attendees. Rebellious flower girl to the right, 1990.*

*Ammah's sixtieth in Bearsden, Glasgow.*

*Appah with his little shadow Dan. First grandchild.*

*Rosh and her beautiful boys.*

*Appah's seventieth. Sam looking like a child possessed.*

*Kilmelford, our holiday home where we meet annually. Our piece of heaven on earth.*

*Galle Face Hotel where we used to stroll and have ice cream on a Sunday. Taken on our 2005 visit.*

*Sri Lankan elephants at Yalla. A finer and gentler species than their human counterparts.*

*Kandy – seat of the Sinhala kings. Buddha's tooth is housed in the temple here.*

Kantheswami Temple in Jaffna – the capital of the Tamil Kings.
The first temple on this site was constructed in 948. This is the fourth built in 1749.

Jaffna College, built in 1867. Many of the Sanders family were educated, and taught, here.

*Mathagal beach ... no swimming permitted, 2005.*

*My great grandfather's house at St John's College scheduled for demolition due to war damage.*

*The Last King of Jaffna, Sankilli II. He fought the Portugese and was exiled to Goa 400 years ago.*

*The ruins of ancient Tamil palaces – several centuries old.*

*Sankilli Thopu. Bullet-ridden archway to palace in Nallur – over 400 years old.*

*My Guru Vasa in 2005. Destroyed by the army.*

*Rev Joseph Sanders' Atchuvaley church built after he secured funding 100 years ago.*

In Loving Memory
of
**REV. JOSEPH MANICKAM SANDERS**
1857—1913
AND WIFE
**EMILY ANNAPILLAI**
1861—1931
AND SON
**DANIEL RAJAH SANDERS**
21. 10. 1895—13. 3. 1921
TEACHER, JAFFNA COLLEGE
*"WE SHALL NOT ALL SLEEP."*

*Tablet in memory of Rev Sanders,*
*Emily and Daniel, who died young.*

*St James's Church Nallur, Jaffna. I was christened here and two of my great-great grandfathers served as ministers in this church.*

*Unkept burial grounds where my ancestors sleep, including my great great grandfather, my great grandfather and my grandfather Iyah, 2005.*

*Simmy is christened, Edinburgh 2005.*

*Appah 1932–2006.*

*Appah's grave smothered with Ammah's flowers.*
*Palm trees on headstone for the man from Ceylon.*

*Appah's Handy cousins, attentive to the end.*

*In Kilmelford with mummy and grandchildren before she fell ill.*

*Rosh wins award for her pioneering work in electronic eye referrals in Scotland. The champagne was great too!*

# ASNEMGE

*The* European Gastroenterology Association

founded in 1947

In appreciation of his outstanding scientific work,

## Dr. David S Sanders

has been selected as a

## Rising Star in Gastroenterology 2010

for his presentation at the UEGW Barcelona 2010.

Prof. Dr. Franco Bazzoli
President ASNEMGE

Prof. Dr. Mark Hull
Secretary General ASNEMGE

Association des Sociétés Nationales Européennes et Méditerranéennes de Gastroentérologie
Association of National European and Mediterranean Societies of Gastroenterology

*Professor D.S. Sanders wins the Rising Star of Europe.*

*I am awarded the Fellowship in General Practice 2007.*

Information for staff

Staff news archive

Staff News

2012 staff news archive

2011 staff news archive

University professor wins national award for groundbreaking coeliac research

University Christmas card released

University unveils new plans to enhance landmark building

The University of Sheffield named University of the Year

Academic raises thousands for Children in Need

University scientist awarded coveted Royal Society Research Fellowship

Professor Richard Dawkins opens £4.3 million University life sciences institute

'Thanks a million' say engineering students

University of Sheffield

## University professor wins national award for groundbreaking coeliac research

Professor David Sanders, a Consultant Gastroenterologist at Sheffield Teaching Hospitals NHS Foundation Trust and the University of Sheffield, has been granted a renowned national award for his research into a common bowel condition.

Professor Sanders has received the Cuthbertson Medal from the Nutrition Society for his contribution to research into coeliac disease. This hereditary disorder of the small intestine is an autoimmune disease, meaning the patient's immune system attacks its own cells and tissues by mistake. It gives the sufferer a heightened sensitivity to gluten.

Professor Sanders has carried out extensive research into coeliac disease and its history, causes, symptoms and treatment.

He was the first investigator to describe the fact that patients presenting with irritable bowel syndrome (IBS) could have previously undetected coeliac disease. This landmark study has changed the way clinicians deal with patients presenting with IBS symptoms and government guidelines now recommend mandatory testing for coeliac disease.

Professor Sanders was presented the award by Professor Ian MacDonald, Professor of Metabolic Physiology at Nottingham University, at the British Association of Parenteral and Enteral Nutrition's (BAPEN) annual congress.

The Cuthbertson Medal is given each year to young scientists for excellence in clinical nutrition research that provides evidence for clinicians to use in their work. Granted annually since 1990 as a tribute to Sir David Cuthbertson, the late nutrition research pioneer, it is recognised as one of the most prestigious awards in the field.

The Coeliac Specialist clinic at the Royal Hallamshire Hospital has the largest population of patients within the UK – more than 1000. But despite this there may be up to 5000 undiagnosed cases in Sheffield alone.

Today, around 1per cent of UK adults are affected by the disease, which can cause chronic diarrhoea, fatigue and growth deficiency as well as other symptoms.

At present, the only known treatment for the disease is a lifelong gluten-free diet. However, this raises uncertainties with the nutritional effects of such a diet, for example on cholesterol levels. It is also not clearly understood whether adult patients with undetected coeliac disease, who also have Type 1 diabetes, benefit from a gluten-free diet.

Much of Professor Sanders recent research has focussed on the nutritional effects of a gluten-free diet as well as the effects of having undetected coeliac disease. With factors such as this in mind, the Professor's research has profound implications for the treatment of patients in the future.

Professor Sanders, who was also named European Rising Star in Gastroenterology in 2010, said: "I'm truly honoured to be awarded this medal and I feel very fortunate."

*David wins the Cuthbertson Medal for his research into coeliac disease.*

*Manie Marmie's eightieth birthday, Austraila 2005.*

*The cousins in Tenerife. 'Hot chick' with hangers on.*

*Rebecca, Rohi's second cousin from Australia.*

*My Uncle Balan and Aunt Susila visit us in 2011.*

*D.S. Sanders IV. Our Little Terror.*

*Simmy takes eco-friendly transport to school.*

*The cousins together – the future.*

*On my morning walk this is what I see.*

*Beautiful, safe Edinburgh.*

# CHAPTER 10

# GOODBYE ISLAND IN THE SUN

My grandfather is in a goldfish bowl in Colombo Hospital. He is tied up with lots of string. We are not allowed to touch him or speak to him. We can only look through the window.

We have all had to come to Colombo, because he had a heart attack. They say the doctors jumped on him nine times, so he is bound to be better now. Coming to Colombo is very exciting because we get to meet all our cousins again, even though it is not Christmas.

The last time we were here was a few months before for the All Ceylon Song Contest with our *Chithappah*, Dad's 'little' brother Balan. Miss Perfect sang 'All Kinds of Everything' and won.

It should have been me, except that I was interrupted in the middle of my song and a step put under me because I was so small and the microphone too far away. There was really no need, as my voice is quite loud. They also put me on very late so I was genuinely sleepy, singing, 'Past Eight o'clock and it's Bedtime for Dolly.' The audience started laughing and it was not meant to be a funny song. These people do not know how to look after small children. If I hadn't been so badly treated, I would definitely have won instead of my sister.

I love travelling around with my *Chithappah*, who causes quite a stir wherever he goes. His skin is pale. He is wearing a white shirt, dark trousers, sun glasses and he is well over six foot, a giant in Lilliput. I can see that all the girls are jealous that I have such a handsome escort.

This time in Colombo someone kind has sent us food and crates of drink. There is a tradition in Ceylon to send food and drink to a bereaved household, as those who grieve, unless you are me, do not tend to eat well.

This upsets my grandmother a lot as Iyah is not dead. Personally I think she is overreacting – no way is he going to die and, if she would only try it, the food is delicious. I have also got the delights of a crate of Vimto and other fizzy drinks that I do not even recognise in front of me.

The adults are speaking in hushed voices but the loudest voice is coming from the phone and sounds like my father shouting!

When I left Jaffna I told the girls I was not coming back and they all gave me presents. Harriet warned me that it was not good to tell lies, as we were only planning to be away for a few weeks but now my story is coming true. I think I must have a special sense. I overhear my Periappah Rajan telling my sister that he may need to take us to live with our parents, because Iyah is very ill.

It would be great fun to go to England. We are all excited about it. When my parents' letters come they are from Queen's Gardens, Edinburgh. I am fairly sure that this is because the Queen comes to live there in the summer. I wonder if she sometimes sits overlooking the lawn and sipping tea. English people love tea, especially our tea. I know that Edinburgh is not London but it's very close by.

The brat brother has no idea what is happening and is very pleased to see my uncle Daniel and aunt Chelvathy. There is a mutual adoration. My grandfather's initials are D.S. Sanders, my uncle was the next D.S. Sanders and my brother the third D.S. Sanders. I think that is why my uncle is so fond of him. There is no other reason to like him.

It is in truly Ceylonese style that my uncle had initials that do not match his name. This is not an attempt at fraud. His full name Daniel Selvarajah Sanders was too much of a mouthful, so everyone called him Rajan.

I have to digress briefly at this point and put in a paragraph about my own name, which I detest. My parents painstakingly chose the name Roshini for their eldest, as it meant 'light'. They took several days to decide what to call her and consulted a number of relatives. In contrast, what to call me took about five minutes, the deciding factor being what rhymed with Roshini.

Nice to know they made such an effort over me from the beginning. No one ever calls me Sureshini unless I am in trouble. The mispronunciation of this name is so frequent, that I practically answer to anything. Worse still the hordes that prefer my sister to me, call me 'Suroshini'.

We were not at all bothered about my grandmother's fervent hugs, boarding the plane or about seeing the palm trees get smaller and smaller and vanish. This was a great adventure. I knew my grandfather would get better and we were sure to be back in a week or two.

On board we were given toffee to chew in case our ears hurt and toys to play with for free, by smiling ladies wearing what looked like army uniform. Our air hostesses wear saris. Meals came on little trays and packets, it was very exciting. I wondered if children in England got all their meals in cartons.

My aunt and uncle were very kind to us and told us we would be going to Paris first to meet our parents and then on to England. We were in no hurry. It would be fun to see the Eiffel Tower and the funny frog-eating people.

All too soon the flight was over and we landed. The brat started screaming and my aunt thought it was because his ears hurt but he was just doing it to get more toffee.

We got to the airport and a lady in a skirt and a black man were waiting for us. They said they were our parents and, though I had seen pictures often, I was not sure. My sister said it was true and that we should kiss them.

We didn't get to see much of Paris as we were only there one night in a hotel before leaving on another plane. In the hotel we ate some cake and accidentally dropped bits on the floor. The parents made us pick it all up, which we thought was just plain mean, as the servants could have done it. They were already telling us what to do and what not to do and my brother and I would check with our sister if the requests were appropriate. She was no help at all, shrugged and said, 'These are your parents, and you have to listen to them now.' On the plus side this meant Miss Bossy was out of a job.

We kept telling our brother that these really were his parents but he clung on to my aunt and did not let go. He had to be prised off like a leech. He really did not get it or understand what was happening. I was beginning to wonder if there was something wrong with him, he seemed a little slow to me.

Then we took another plane and after a very short journey, there it was: London. Vast, sprawling, glistening with lights and buildings packed together, 'Why', I thought to myself, 'London alone looks the size of Ceylon.'

*Rev. Joseph Sanders 1857–1913.
My Sanders great grandfather.*

*Rev.C.C.Handy, Principal of St Johns College. My Handy
great grandfather. His picture still hangs in the College.*

*Harriet Handy with sister-in-law. My grandmother standing.*

91

*Rev J.T. Handy MBE. Dad looked more like his Handy uncles than a Sanders.*

*Handy cousins – 1930s.*

*Dad front right and siblings – 1937.*

*D.S. Sanders Inspector of American Mission Schools. My grandfather 'Iyah' 1892–1980.*

*D.S. Sanders – second row, 3rd left, Vice Principal of Jaffna College.*

DR. S. L. NAVARATNAM

## GIFT OF ONE MONTH'S SALARY

MR. A.R. ABRAHAM
MR. P.W. ARIARATNAM
MR. S. ARIATHURAI
MR. T.P.H. ARULAMPALAM
MR. S. BALARAMAN
MR. S.V. BALASINGHAM
MR. J.S. BATES
MR. R.S.B. BEADLE
MR. A.M. BRODIE
REV. S.K. BUNKER
MISS P. CHELLIAH
MRS R.T. DAVID
MR. V. EHAMPARAM
MR. C.O. ELIAS
MR. K.A. GEORGE
MR. K.V. GEORGE
MR. S.K. GNANAMUTTU
MR. S.T. JEEVARATNAM
MR. P. JEEVARATNAM

MR. A.S. PONNAMBALAM
MR. H.N. PONNAMBALAM
MISS L. PONNAMBALAM
MR. T. PONNAMPALAM
MR. C.S. PONNUTHURAI
MRS I. PONNUDURAI
MR. M.A. RAJARATNAM
MRS T. RAMANATHAN
MRS R. RATNAM
MR. C.R. RATNASINGHAM
MR. D.S. SANDERS
MR. S.S. SANDERS
MR. S. SATCHITHANANTHAM
MR. K. SELLAIAH
MR. K.A. SELLIAH
MR. J.A. SELVADURAI
MR. J. SINNAPPAH
MR. B.K. SOMASUNDRAM
MR. A.C. SUNDRAMPILLAI

*The Sanders brothers gift a months salary towards school projects.*

*Mrs C.C. Handy, my great grandmother and dad behind her. His cousin Kanthi on her knee.*

*The Sanders family minus Rajan in hiding, Jaffna 1940s.*

*Manie, dad's eldest sister and Kanagarajah courting at Colombo University 1950s.*

*Manie's wedding. Guru Vasa 1953 Jaffna.*

*Appah and Rajan at Rajan's wedding 1959.*

*Chandra, Dad's second sister.*

*Chandra, Jaffna College Pianist.*

*Chandra Marmie's wedding, 1956.*

*Chandra Marmie, Ratnarajah Uncle
and cousins with Appammah.*

*Dad's Basket Ball Championship Team 1949. Back row, 3rd from left.*

*Dad at Colombo University, 1951–56.*  *Balan, Dad's handsome 'little' brother.*

Name : S C Sanders

Date of Birth : July 1st 1932

Date of Registration
as Medical Student : June 2nd 1951

*The two brothers, on holiday in Guru Vasa.*

*Dad's gormless med student pass.*

*The Brodie Hostel Bunch 1952. Dad with moustache front row 3rd right.
Professor Eliezer, cousin by marriage, in the middle.*

*My favourite picture of Appah fishing in the Indian Ocean 1959.*

*Ship's Doctor KK's with the boys, before Ammah put an end to all the fun.*

*Ammah working on the TB ward.*

*The Most Beautiful Girl in the World.*

*Appah and Ammah gallivanting before marriage.*

*Ammah is Christened 'Irene'.*

*Sitting on the back steps, Jaffna.*

*The family at Guru Vasa, 1960.*

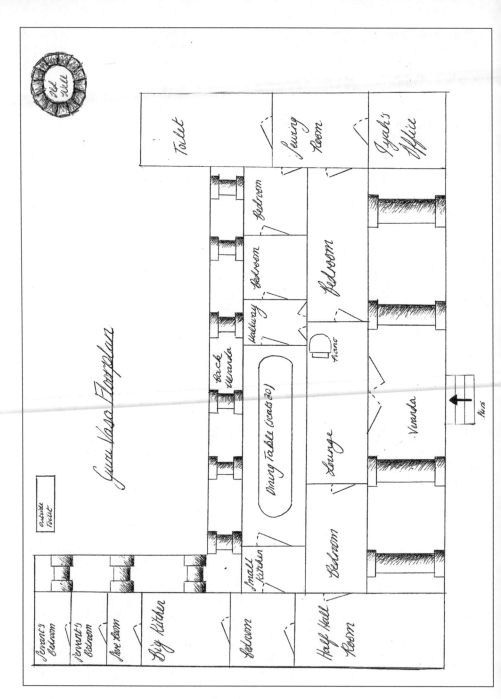

*Floor plan of Guru Vasa.*

*Iyah Appammah, Manie Marmie and cousins sitting on the verandah at Guru Vasa.
A typical Ceylon afternoon on the porch.*

*Rosh on Appammah's lap. The last picture of all the family in Guru Vasa, 1962.*

*Happy parents.*

*Ammah and Rosh, see how happy they look.*

*The grandparents, cousins and Rosh, Guru Vasa.*

*Ammah and me. I think she is about to drop me.*

*The three of us taken by a tall photographer. We look as if we are sliding downhill.*

*Family photo, Colombo 1968.*

*Family photo before our parents left us.*

105

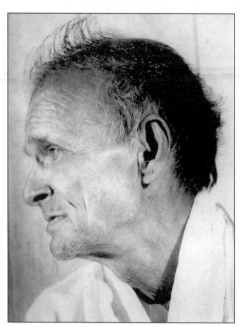

*The three of us after our parents left, 1970.*

*Our Sara grandfather Appu before he died.*

*Family gathering as another cousin is born.*

*David's Birthday, Ranee in skirt and Kantheswami with metal cap extreme left.*

*Sara grandmother seated, Ranee and various 'German' cousins.*

*Nesi in contemplation.*

*Don Juan Wickremaratne.*

*Nesi and Wicky.*

*My cousin Siri, 1960s.*

*My aunt Ranee and cousins. She was more like one of us than our parents' generation.*

*Ranee in Sari Tamil style.*

*Ranee in Sari Sinhala style
when she won her beauty contest.*

*Thusha dressed as a doctor for a school play. Innocent happier times before Civil War destroyed her life.*

*Ammah's only brother Rajadhurai
refused to leave Sri Lanka.*

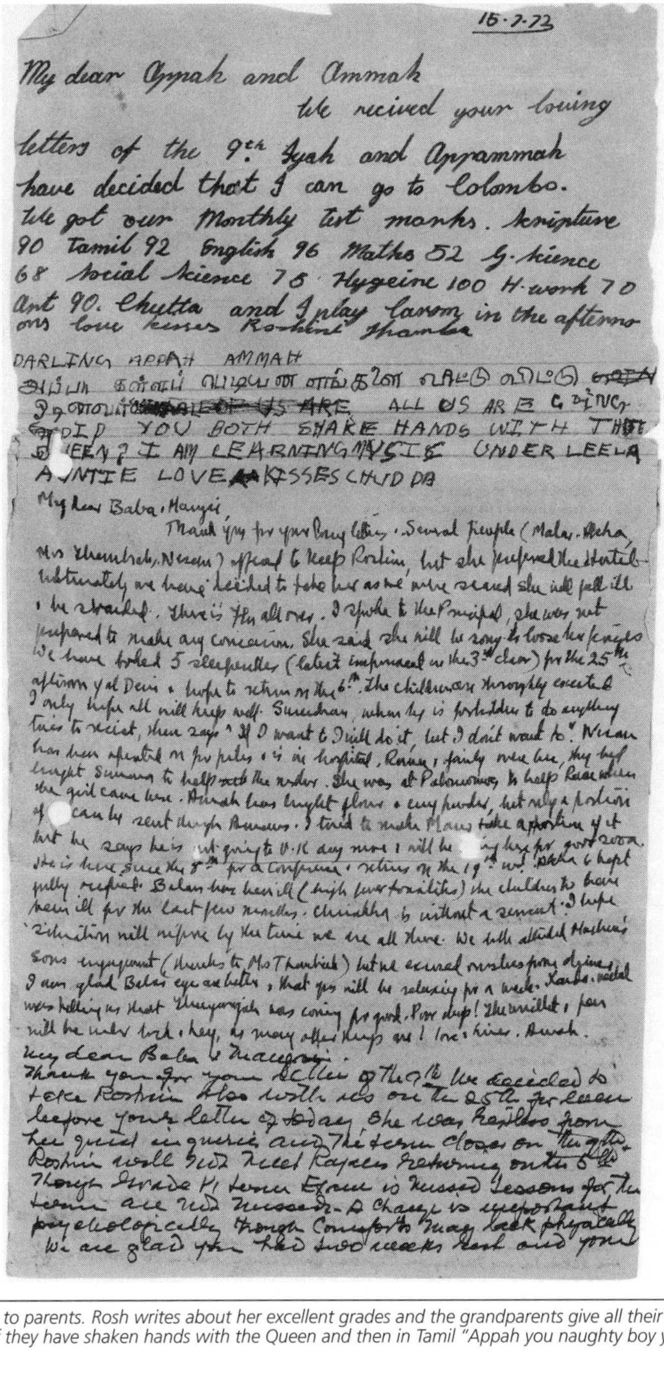

15.7.72

My dear Appah and Ammah
We recived your loving letters of the 9th. Ayah and Appammah have decided that I can go to Colombo. We got our Monthly test marks. Scripture 90 tamil 92 English 96 Maths 52 G. Science 68 Social Science 78 Hygeine 100 H. work 70 Art 90. Chutta and I play Carom in the afternoons love kisses Roshini Thambo

DARLING APPAH AMMAH
[illegible]
~~[illegible] ALL OF US ARE~~ ALL US ARE GOING
DID YOU BOTH SHAKE HANDS WITH THE QUEEN? I AM LEARNING MUSIC UNDER LEELA AUNTIE LOVE KISSES CHUDDA

My dear Baba, Mangai,
Thank you for your long letters. Several people (Mala, Asha, Mrs Thambiah, Nesam) offered to keep Roshini, but she preferred the Hostel. Ultimately we have decided to take her as we were scared she will fall ill & be stranded. There is flu all over. I spoke to the Principal, she was not prepared to make any concession. She said she will be sorry to loose her [illegible]. We have booked 5 sleepers (latest improvement in the 3rd class) for the 25th afternoon yal Devi & hope to return on the 6th. The children are thoroughly excited. I only hope all will keep well. Surendran, when he is forbidden to do anything tries to resist, then says "If I want to I will do it, but I don't want to". Nesam has been operated on for piles & is in hospital. Rosary & family were here, they had brought Sumana to help with the [illegible]. She was at Palamunai, to help Rasa when the girl came here. Ammah has bought flour & curry powder, but only a portion of it can be sent through Ramesus. I tried to make Mano take a portion of it but he says he is not going to U.K any more & will be [illegible] here for good soon. He is here since the 8th for a Conference & returns on the 19th. [illegible] & hope fully recuperate. Balan has been ill (high fever tonsilitis) the children too have been ill for the last few months. Chinthy is without a servant. I hope situation will improve by the time we are all there. We both attended Mahesan's sons engagement (thanks to Mrs Thambiah) but we excused ourselves from dining. I am glad Bala's eyes are better, & that you will be relaxing for a week. [illegible] was telling us that Thiagarajah was coming for good. Poor chap! The millet & [illegible] will be [illegible] & [illegible], as many other things are! Love & kisses. Ammah.

My dear Bala & Mangai,
Thank you for your letter of the 7th. We decided to take Roshini also with us on the 25th for leave before your letter of today. She was [illegible] from her [illegible] and the term closes on the [illegible]. Roshini will [illegible] Rajees returning on the 6th. Though Grade VI term Exam is missed Lessons for the term are not missed. A change is important psychologically though comforts may lack physically. We are glad you had two weeks rest and your

Letter to parents. Rosh writes about her excellent grades and the grandparents give all their news.
I ask them if they have shaken hands with the Queen and then in Tamil "Appah you naughty boy you left me".

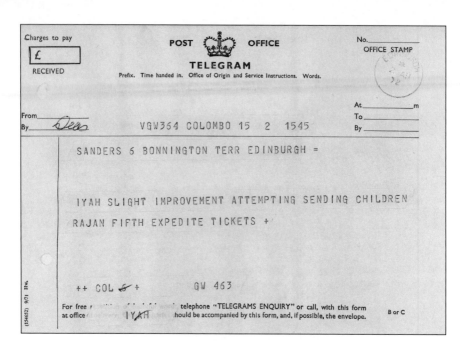

*Telegram 1972.*

CHAPTER 11

# PAVED WITH GOLD

Dick Whittington turned out to be a liar. As soon as we landed, we could see it. The streets of London were not paved with gold. It was freezing and wet and the people were so big that they made us feel invisible.

Edinburgh was nowhere near London and Queen's Gardens was a dump. To be precise, it was more like the Edinburgh Dungeon than a Queen's residence. We stayed way at the top in the attic and Appah could only stand in the middle of the room. He kept forgetting this fact and would bump his head and curse which was not setting a good example for us children.

There were only two rooms for us – a bedroom and everything else. My sister said nothing, but my brother and I were beginning to suspect that we had been kidnapped by these people. We had woken to a nightmare.

The food was awful and barely adequate and, as there were no servants, we had to keep cleaning up after ourselves. There wasn't even a *dobbie*, so we had to go to a common wash house and wait until our clothes were cleaned. It was so cold that I hardly took my coat off, even in the flat. I reassured myself that I would be leaving soon, best to keep the coat on and be ready.

Nothing, however, prepared me for the joys of my new school. Having switched from Sinhala to Tamil, now everything was in English. I spoke well but my reading and writing were way behind.

The school was an austere Victorian building with wooden seats and a belt for the badly behaved. No more the open plan classrooms of Ceylon. I was to be locked away and forced to learn things.

The teachers were all very understanding and patient with me but my class-mates were evil. There was a set of twins in particular who would beat me up every playtime. My new parents told me it was rude to hit and swear, so I became the human punch bag. People would rub my brown forearm and could not believe that the dirt would not come off. If this was not bad enough, I then had the privilege of remedial classes to set me further apart from the others.

My sister would meet me in the playground and say, 'Stop crying Chutta', which means little sweet, 'come and play with me'. I think she and her friends would have been bored without me. They found me funny.

I complained to my father about my hideous time at school and he told me the tale of the snake:

*The snake was hated by all in the village because it kept biting people. When God was walking in the garden he found him sulking under the shade of the coconut palm.*

*'What's wrong?' God asked.*

*'Everyone hates me', said the snake.*

*'That is because you keep biting everyone. If you are unreasonable and keep doing this, people will hate you'.*

*So the snake decided to be better behaved and the next time God was walking in the garden he came upon him nearly beaten to death.*

*'What happened to you?' He asked.*

*'It's all your fault', hissed the snake. 'You told me not to bite and so they came from the village with sticks and beat me.'*

*'Foolish snake. I told you not to bite but I did not tell you not to stand tall and hiss and shake.'*

Now this sort of parental advice is completely unhelpful to a child. I really did not understand what he was on about and there were clearly no snakes in Edinburgh, were there?

There had been interesting developments with the brat, who now seemed to be everyone's pet and had a lot of friends and no problems at school. He had stopped screaming all the time and was eating like a little pig.

The only good thing about living in Edinburgh was the television and the BBC. We had great respect for the BBC in Ceylon and believed that if anyone told you the truth, it was the BBC. If we really wanted to know what was going on in the world, or even in our own back yard, that was where we tuned into on our radios. We had no television in Guru Vasa, only an old large wireless. Here was something even better – talking and moving pictures in your own home. I even liked the girl with the blackboard and toys who came on when it was time to switch off.

The highlight of the week was pocket money; ten whole pence for sweets and treats. There was a newsagent's on the way to school and he had jars and jars of sweets, cream coloured mice, pink bon-bons, and chocolate éclairs. You picked up a small white paper bag and, after much debate and decision making, measured out your quota. If you were lucky you could get more and if you were unlucky you had to put some back with your grubby paws. My sister always gobbled hers up fast and my brother gave most of his away. I kept mine in a secret place, they lasted longer that way.

Cadbury's was everywhere to be seen, with toffee, without, with mallow, with mint cream. This shop made the *kuddai* across from Guru Vasa look like a slum. I did not realise what I had been missing all these years. I promised myself that if I had stomach space, never again would fruits cross my lips, when such sweeter delights were to be had.

My parents, instead of being pleased to have us with them, seemed in a state of agitation. My father had decided to study for his physician membership exams as well and they were trying to work out when my mother should have her operation. This was all quite needless, as she kept telling us she was fine but he was emphatic that this should be done in the UK, which was the centre of medical excellence. Now, we children knew that just was not true and that Colombo hospital and all things Ceylonese were better. After all, my grandfather had made a full recovery there, as we knew he would, and gone home to Guru Vasa.

Even with my mother working, there was not enough money. We thought that grown-ups were quite greedy and needed a lot. Instead of studying and playing with us, our father decided to get a job. We never knew what was coming next and we children did not entirely trust our parents and stuck together.

Dad's new job meant that we moved to Glasgow and got a hospital bungalow, which was very nice. My brother David had his own room again and I shared with my sister. The house had a lovely large garden and pink rose bushes in the front. The odd thing about this house was that our garden was surrounded with barbed wire. We thought this a little strange.

We had failed to grasp that we had landed in Drumchapel, which was not the most salubrious part of Glasgow. We liked the bungalow because the hospital was at the top of the road, so Dad could pop in at lunchtime and we could see him at work if we wanted. Better still, Ammah soon stopped working and the food situation got much better. The doctors and nurses all treated us with great kindness and best of all were meals out in the hospital canteen. They made jelly with four different colours and it tasted like heaven.

Sadly, even here I had to go to school. I had the good fortune to be seated next to a lovely boy called Steven and made friends with a blonde girl called Caroline. Caroline's father worked in a bakery and she would invite me home and we would stuff ourselves with the most amazing cream cakes and buns. I had discovered another national treasure – Greggs.

There was also the class bully called Gary who stood a foot taller than everyone. Once again I was subject to physical and verbal abuse but at least this time my friends would weakly cry out, 'Stoap aht ya wee bully!'

Trust me he was not 'wee'.

One day I decided that I had had enough and that the pacifist, eastern snake thing was not working for me. I walked up to Gary and punched him right in the face. Once I discovered that I was quite good at punching, I used this technique liberally. My mother was then called for by the teacher and told that she had received several complaints about my behaviour in the playground. She didn't even try to stand up for me, which is what mothers are supposed to do.

I started to enjoy school and if I didn't feel like going, I just vanished to a friend's for a bit. No one seemed to notice, the freedom was enormous.

My sister was not so lucky. She was in senior school and getting a hard time as the only coloured girl in the class trying to study. Being less violent than me when her 'Gary' hit her in the face, she did not retaliate. She brought the odd friend home but one of them stole her watch and a few other things, so she stopped inviting them. This was a far cry from Ladies College Colombo and though deeply unhappy she kept her troubles to herself.

My sister and I used to call Ammah 'Dad's girlfriend'. She certainly did not feel like much of a mother to me. She would hang off his arm and constantly giggle. Mothers should be more serious minded in our opinion. She kept inviting friends over and having coffee mornings and eating cake.

Three ladies who frequented our house were Margaret, Florence and Jane. Margaret was the best of mother's friends and was the local GP's wife. She would tell me really helpful things like, 'Try not to have too many classmates round to the house dear.' Margaret had two daughters who were much older than us but Brian was David's age, as was Jane's son Andrew. We would form quite a gang and run around the vast hospital grounds playing Cops and Robbers or Cowboys and Indians. We provided great entertainment for the patients when they came out to the gardens to get a bit of fresh air.

Caroline came over to play too and we would have picnics by the 'Donny Osmond' tree and imagine what it would be like to be Mrs Osmond. We were obsessed with his music and played 'Puppy Love' repeatedly on our tape recorder.

I missed playing with my father but was very helpful to him as a human clock. He worked long hours and studied in between and would lock himself in a room upstairs to do so. I would sit outside the door on the steps and say,

'It's seven o'clock can you play now?'

'It's eight o'clock can you play now?'

'It's nine o'clock can you come out? I'm going to bed now.'

My mother would eventually drag me away saying, 'Appah has to study *pillai*.'

'No he doesn't, I'm fed up of this and I want to go home', I would grumble.

We had fallen into a routine of work and school and study. We knew no other Ceylonese but the hospital quarters were full of doctors from all nationalities coming and going and our parents being outgoing and friendly made a lot of friends. We also got to sample Greek, Ghanaian and Iranian food.

One year a Sinhalese family came next door for a few months and this was food to the fasting. Most importantly they even had a son about my brother's age. Those days were days of great freedom and we would wander about and play in a way the current generation seems unable to do. This doctor later went back to Sri Lanka and eventually became a professor. My father and he formed a sort of study group with some others, as my father had now passed forty and found it very hard to study. He had missed much of his basic medical training at the start of his career, which now came back to haunt him and he had a lot of catching up to do.

One time, my father took me into town by himself for some reason and it was the best treat ever. We walked everywhere and I skipped along his side and he bought me sweets and a toy. I think it must have been for my birthday. I wanted to walk all the way home but it was getting dark and he insisted we take the bus. Sadly, we had a fall out at this point, as I wanted to prolong the one-to-one experience, which was so rare, and keep walking instead of taking the bus that would get us home sooner.

Appah was quite idealistic at times. When my sister needed a swimsuit, he took her to Jenners and bought her one, even though we had no money. He said this was like Cargills in Ceylon, which is where we would have gone, had we been home. The item was way over his budget, but this did not seem to perturb him.

He bought the most thoughtful gifts and one year my brother got a fantastic robot for Christmas that did all sorts of things. I had a great time playing with it on Christmas Eve but accidentally broke it. I put it back in its box carefully and boy did he get into trouble for his careless behaviour on Christmas Day. I felt a bit bad but another time he had smashed a window with his bow and arrow and didn't tell, so I thought it sort of evened out.

Appah and Ammah made everything into a party. If something bad happened, we had butter cake and Coke to cheer us up and if something good happened, we did it all again but with more gusto.

The façade only dropped at Christmas when we really could not bear the absence of family. We had no holidays abroad and no one from Ceylon came to visit, as foreign travel was unaffordable to most people then.

The next thing to happen was that mother got word to go to Liverpool for her operation and my father wanted to be with her. Once again we were a problem. Dad had a great friend called Francis Balmer, who worked with him briefly, and Francis and his wife, Mary, offered to take us. This was no mean feat, especially because they also had a toddler of their own. We had a week with them in Balloch, which felt like a great vacation. Poor Mary must have been exhausted looking after us but never complained. She was an artist and I loved to see her drawings and paintings. They were such wonderfully kind people, ever mindful of all our needs. Francis had been out in Africa and had to return home in a hurry because he refused to give the whites vaccines before the blacks. In his brief time there he had managed to upset quite a few of the establishment.

Appah came for us a week later and told us that the operation had gone well but that Ammah would have to remain in Liverpool for a month. We returned home to find that we had been burgled and there was a letter from the Ceylon government saying Appah had to return post haste.

My father did not understand what was going on, as he still had a few months of his scholarship left. He wrote to them straight away and explained this and that as he had now passed all his exams, he was quite prepared to return early but for the fact that his wife lay recovering in hospital after a seven-hour surgical procedure.

Their response was that they were not interested in his domestic situation and that if he did not return he risked disciplinary proceedings.

My father then phoned his friends in London.

'They want to axe you because you are a Tamil man, if you are not Sinhala and Buddhist you are out. They are just looking for an excuse.'

I would listen carefully to my father's conversations and cry, 'I want to go home.' I think that helped to focus his mind. My brother did not seem to care and my sister kept quiet, which was annoying. Did no one mind but me? If we had to leave Ammah for a few months in the UK on her own, she was sure to cope. Why the hospital did everything for her, it was like being in a hotel.

We took weekly trips to Liverpool to see Ammah who was back to the crying/kissing thing again. She even told one of the pretty nurses to marry Dad and look after us if she died, which seemed a great over reaction to me!

We loved Dad looking after us because there were very few rules and we got a two meats and no veg diet every day. We stayed up late, watched what we liked on TV and wandered into the hospital whenever we wanted to see him, for endless supplies of chocolate and Coke readily available in the canteen.

Dad then got another government letter telling him he was blacklisted and that they had vacated his post, since he was not returning. In short he did not have a job to go home to and did indeed face disciplinary action. I thought this was fair enough, as they had warned us. I was angry with my mother, it was all her fault.

A second angel came at this time of darkness and his name was David Ross. He was one of those tough old school gents and reminded me of Iyah. Dr Ross told Dad that he should move out of the Drumchapel doctor's quarters and apply for a senior registrar's post now that he had completed his exams. The battle with the government could take years to resolve and the concern was that Dad was putting his children's education and future at risk. The SR post meant more money and Dr Ross advised that he should buy a home, however small, in Bearsden where the local non-fee paying school was excellent.

So that is what we did. Ammah came home, Appah got his SR post and we bought a small semi-detached house in Bearsden. We kept our suitcases over the wardrobe even after we moved in and did not buy too much in case we had to leave for Ceylon in a hurry. Appah continued regular communication with the government to explain his situation. Sooner or later a letter from the government was bound to come saying they had made a mistake, meanwhile we would make the best of it and live.

My mother looked different after her operation, better, so we travelled the length and breadth of Britain taking photographs and enjoying the beauty and varied scenery. They bought an electric blue Chrysler Alpine car with a tape deck and we would play the Beatles, the Shadows and Cliff Richard and sing along the way.

'When we go home, Iyah and Appammah will love to see these pictures. We'll have a family slide show of all the wonderful places we visited in Britain', Appah said.

# CHAPTER 12

# A BLACK MAN

My father was in an awkward position. Letters still kept going to and from the Sri Lankan government and they were taking a very tough stance with him, telling him he had no post to go back to. He even paid back every penny of his scholarship money, in case they held that against him too.

He passed the membership (Member of the Royal College of Physicians, MRCP) and then decided to move away from forensic medicine; after all he was only doing it because the government had allocated him this speciality.

Care of the elderly was then a new speciality and the concept that older patients should be treated differently quite a revolutionary idea. They reacted to surgery and drugs in a different way from younger people and needed specialised nursing care and often the support of physiotherapists, speech therapists and occupational therapists. Dad thought that this was a holistic branch of medicine that he would enjoy. He also felt guilty about abandoning his parents, so at least he could try to help someone else's. These patients generally had many things wrong with them and their complex needs were a challenge to unravel.

He was taken under the wing of Sir Ferguson Anderson, who later became the world's first professor of geriatric medicine.

He thrived in this speciality but then hit a bit of a brick wall, as many felt that appointing a foreigner as a consultant would be a 'black day' for medicine in Glasgow. Many of those at his level were jealous of him and there were plenty of petty and irritating stories, presentations where his slides mysteriously disappeared, colleagues using his cases and stealing his ideas as their own. Hospital medicine was and is brutally competitive, so I am sure other doctors have similar stories but his own boss told him that there was a colour bar.

A prestigious consultant's post came up in a teaching hospital in Glasgow and David Ross encouraged him to apply for this. There were several applicants including a local consultant's daughter, who clearly thought she had the job. When the interviews were all complete the candidates sat outside in a row awaiting the verdict. Much dispute was overheard and then David Ross emerged, harassed, from the room and asked my father,

'Sam, are you Catholic?'

'No', came the response.

'Thank God for that, I can swing everything else but that really would have been the end of you!'

We are so very correct and careful today in our interviews and selection processes. I would like to think we are more open minded, or are we just more careful and less transparent?

My father had at last found his vocation and in 1975, at the old age of forty-three, was appointed as a consultant. He loved it all, the ward rounds, the house visits, liaising with General Practitioners and relatives. He gradually built a solid team around him and they were each valued and unique in what they offered.

Some of his patients were regulars and he got to know them quite well. This branch of medicine also had some continuity of care, unlike many other specialties which felt a bit like a conveyer belt system.

Once he went to visit an elderly lady at home and after he had taken a history and examined her she said:

'You sound just like my dad.'

My father was beginning to wonder if he had seriously misjudged her and was contemplating a mental function test when she explained that her father had been a sailor from Ceylon. She looked quite pale and Caucasian so he would never have guessed it.

Part of my job is sometimes to run courses for doctors and I tell them, 'We are all geriatricians now' as our population is living longer and by 2030 a third of us will be over sixty-five. Like my father, I too have a passion for this part of my job, as there is much work to be done for our senior citizens, who often need help and are the last to ask for it.

Appah was also asked to become an elder at the church, so he would minister to these patients' physical and spiritual needs on some occasions.

Our minister was a free-spirited young man who wore jeans, had long hair and drove a sports car. My father appreciated his unique messages and was pleased that he attracted a lot of young people to the church. Many of the older members of the congregation were not quite so taken with him, and the minister had a long battle bringing them round.

I thought that the minister was always staring at me in church and it took me a while to realise that he was actually looking at the graceful girl behind me, whom he later married.

One Sunday, another well-meaning elder in church introduced Dad to a Kenyan man who was visiting and said,

'Ah Sam, you two will have a lot in common, coming from the same part of the world as you do.'

We fell about laughing hysterically, but Dad did not find it very funny.

As time passed, a steady dribble of Tamil Ceylonese started to settle in Glasgow. These doctors were generally very much younger than my parents and so they felt the need to help them, as their friends had done when they first arrived. They fully understood the homesickness and confusion of new migrants.

They helped their fellow countrymen with advice and references and had several dinner parties. In the early days of these gatherings we really had a good time. At Christmas, all were invited and small gifts were given to each and every person. Around thirty people were catered for on Christmas Day, for several years. Eventually we three kids got together and said, 'No more.' We wanted a family Christmas and were sick of assisting in all the cooking and cleaning.

It was a real treat to go to someone's house and have Ceylonese food and talk of familiar places and listen to *Baila* music. This music is a sort of Asian Portuguese mix; it is not really that great but it was ours.

Someone would know someone who had come from Ceylon and so we started to get stories of government brutality and violence against Tamils. Some of the young felt that their elders had let them down; all talk, talk ,talk but no action. These youngsters then decided to take up arms, heralding the beginnings of the Tiger movement.

This then led to much debate in our little expat community. Most were pro-Tiger. They wanted to form a Ceylon Tamil Association (CTA) and elect my father as president.

My father's attitude to this was probably best described by the quote by Groucho Marks:

'Please accept my resignation. I do not want to belong to any club that will accept people like me as a member.'

Famous politicians like Amirthalingam and Sivasithamparam came home for dinner and talked for hours on how to find a peaceful solution. My father knew them and shared their moderate views.

Appah was very different from these other Glasgow Ceylonese because he was older than them, had lived amongst the Sinhalese and still had many Sinhalese friends. If you do not live with a people it is easy to vilify them and turn against them. He was a man of strong Christian faith, his grandfathers on both sides had been ministers and he did not believe in violence.

Civil war was rumbling along and refugees were emerging from the chaos with horror stories. My father then started writing to the British government and the newspapers. He gave interviews and was the voice of reason in a sea of madness.

The CTA decided to collect money for the refugees and my parents donated generously.

Later Dad found out that some of this money had gone to the Tiger movement and he publicly denounced the Glasgow CTA. He was livid, as he had been clear about his stance. He demanded that every penny he had given should go to supporting the refugees, not towards funding violence.

He shouted at the others, calling them 'armchair politicians'. They could sit in the safety of their British homes playing politics and sending innocents to their death.

No one dared challenge him overtly but we got fewer invites to dinner and gradually we drifted away from this group and kept to our Scottish friends. Poor Dad was on his own island once again. This whole episode deeply upset him and he felt both betrayed and furious. He used to play Harry Belafonte's song:

*This is my island in the sun*
*where my people have toiled since time begun*
*I may sail on many a sea*
*Her shores will always be home to me*

*Oh island in the sun*
*Willed to me by my father's hand*
*All my days I will sing in praise*
*of your forest, waters and shining sand*

I have in my possession a speech my father gave at a meeting in 1990 and have copied it, as it so clearly portrays the Sri Lankan problem and his position and thoughts on the situation. My father was a fighter and an optimist in many ways, but this speech has a degree of desperation and hopelessness to it and sadly was a premonition of what was to come.

Transcript on the following pages.

Glasgow 8.12.90

*Hamish Law*
*Colinsay*

During recent times we have seen momentous changes in our world. Changes occurring at a speed which we could not have forseen and changes altering the future of countries, continents and the whole world. Nelson Mandela has been released and South Africa has committed itself to dismantling the Apartheid system. The Berlin wall has come down and we have a unified Germany. With the blessings of President Gorbachov the politics of USSR and Eastern European countries is changing rapidly towards a unified Europe and disarmament. More recently the Iraq/Kwait issue with the threat of war and nearer home the replacement of a long-standing Prime Minister in Britain have been dominating issues in the media. In the midst of these major events the fate of a few million civilians in a small island barely 200mls by 300mls somewhere in the Indian Ocean could be deemed a trivial issue of little world impact.

But for many of us assembled here today this was our Island in the Sun and these are our people, and all the major events thru the plight of our people dominate our minds.

2.

Though the media give vast coverage to important issues and the Sri Lankan problem barely gets a mention we are deeply grateful that Humanitarian Organisations like Amnesty International and the Red Cross and interested Politicians, Academics, Religious Dignitaries and Leaders continue their sustained interest in the Human Rights Campaign in Sri Lanka. We thank the organisers of this meeting and those present to lend their support. Above all we thank Amnesty International for its Worldwide Sri Lankan Campaign over the last quarter of 1990 which in itself speaks for the gross violations of Human Rights endured by our people.

2.     When I left Ceylon, as it was still called then, it was a beautiful island with coconut palms swaying in the wind, sun-kissed beaches filled with tourists and tea and rubber plantations flourishing in the hills. With democracy firmly implanted, improving economy and standards of living, good schools and universities with 95% literacy of the population, good Western and Indigenous medical care and the second largest economic growth rate in Asia, Ceylon was destined to become the next marvel in Asia second to Singapore. The people were largely friendly and deeply religious. Whether they were Buddhists, Hindus, Moslems or Christians they abhorred violence and lived in harmony - although -

3.

and lived in harmony—although already seeds of violence and hatred were were being sown by politicians with their own welfare at heart, bringing up issues like race, religion & language. The country was variously called "The Pearl of the Indian Ocean","Isle of Paradise" or the "Garden of Eden" Today; and particularly over the past 7 years, once the serpent has crept into the Garden of Eden, all hell has been let loose in Paradise and Sri Lanka is more a large tear drop than a pearl in the Indian Ocean. Respect for human life has been lost by the State as well as its opponents law & order has all but disappeared, the country is in economic ruin and hatred & violence have replaced harmony.

It is not for us to discuss the rights and wrongs of actions or to dissect the political wisdom of events or leaders involved. I do however, believe in the words of John Lindsay who said: "Those who uphold the law must be wiser and calmer than those who seek to repudiate it". Our main concern is for the suffering of our Tamil People principally in the North & East of Sri Lanka, living without basic amenities like food, clothing & shelter, living without basic Human Rights and living in constant danger of their lives due to regular indiscriminate attack by the Govt armed forces and Home Guards armed by the State.

4.

I would like to review in particular the position and feelings of the civilian Tamil population living in Sri Lanka and our own position living in various countries, far away from our kith and kin.

The Tamils of Sri Lanka are under continuous seige, forced to live like rodents or rabbits rather than human beings, spending large part of their lives underground. Small children with their sharp ears: shout the warning : "Heli, Heli" at the sound approaching Helicopters and all scurry into their bunkers. Those not so speedy, specially the sick, the old, children and women, are killed or maimed by indiscriminate helicopter strafing, aerial bombing or naval & ground force shelling which follows on Nepam bombs set fire to homes, official premises and ancient monuments. Temples, churches and hospitals are not exempt. In addition, civilians become the victims of killing, torture or rape during moves of armed force through towns and villages. Thousands of people have become refugees due to loss of their dwellings or danger in their areas. In the over-flowing churches, schools and refugee camps they are not safe either, subjected to attacks from the armed forces or ~~Home guards~~. *Vigilante Groups.*

5.

Wherever they are they live without electricity, without fuel and with acute shortage of food. Hospitals have been destroyed by shelling and bombing and medicines have run out. People die of remediable illnesses due to the lack of medical facilities, lack of transport and danger involved in seeking out hospitals further afield. In the improvised refugee camps air and water borne infections are running rife with no medicines for prevention or cure. Money, even for dire needs, is not an available commodity as banks are closed, offices for payment of salaries and benefits are closed and even post offices where postal orders sent by relatives abroad ~~could be cashed~~ could be cashed are closed. There is no schooling, no transport, no mail or telephone communication and no access to independent observers or impartial media. They survive isolated and bury ~~their~~ or cremate their dead in silence or with weeping – if they can find the bodies – as the State allows incarceration, execution and disposal of bodies without trial or inquest.

This, ladies and gentlemen, is the plight of a race which 20 years ago was affluent, educated and taking a leading part in the affairs of the country.

6.

To those of us living in Britain and other countries the position of our nearest kith and kin living in Sri Lanka is a continuous psychological torture. We receive no letters or when we receive one by circuitous routes we do not know whether the writer is still living or dead. Last month one of my friends, a consultant hospital doctor, telephoned me in tears. He had heard down the grapevine that his mother had died. When she died, how she died or when she was buried were all unknown. He could only gather friends and relatives and hold a memorial service for her. We are not able to telephone them. We are unable to travel to their aid, or merely to see them or attend a family function, as transport to the North and East has been cut off and alternative transport is fraught with danger. We read distorted and often opposing news in the newspapers, and obituaries like "Killed by a bomb" or "Died under tragic circumstances" frequently. To a large extent our arms are paralysed and we do the best we can under the circumstances to give as much publicity as possible to the plight of our people and render whatever help we can to alleviate their suffering.

7.

Where do we go from here ? I frankly doubt that if left only to the resources of the Government and contending parties there will be a soluti to the problem in the forseeable future. Much can be done and there is much to be done and we look to all sympathetic countries in the world to take part.

Of immediate and vital importance is refugee aid to the affected peo particularly food, medicines and clothing. There is some evidence recentl that the Government embargo on these is easing. Churches have been allowe limited convoys of lorries to transport aid parcels from Colombo and the International Red Cross Organisation has been allowed into the area to he in the distribution of aid and to set up medical centres and rebuild and reopen the main General Hospital.

It is also important to continue the impetus of giving world-wide publicity to the plight of the people and the gross violation of Human Rights. Groups within Sri Lanka like Peoples Forums, Citizens Rights Grou Religous and Ecumenical Groups and the University Teachers HUMAN RIGHTS Group find it difficult and dangerous to collect data and make their voices heard. Of t last group we remember with sadness and respect Dr.Rajani Thiranagama, Lecturer at the Jaffna Medical Faculty who was cruelly gunned down in her prime for her tireless and impartial pursuit of breaches of human rights committed by all parties concerned.

8.

It is more for us living abroad to publicise the issue wherever we are. It is pleasing in recent times to hear of concerns voiced by the EEC, Scandinavian countries, United States, Canada and Australia among others but this is not enough. *to turn the tide.*

The Government of Sri Lanka is very much sustained by foreign aid from the IMF and World Bank and there are even allegations that some of the aid is being surreptiously used to purchase more arms and ammunition. These agencies are in a powerful position to suspend aid until Human Right are re-established in Sri Lanka. It would also be important thereafter to monitor the progress in Human Rights before re-starting aid programs. We are encouraged that the UN Subcommittee on disappearances and Human Rights intend visiting Sri Lanka in February 1991. We also find encouragem in the Commonwealth Initiative headed by the Australian Prime Minister Bob Hawke, though this has yet to elicit favourable response from the Sri Lankan Government.

We , the Tamils of Sri Lanka, continue look to the Nations of the world to use their influence to bring a peaceful solution to the problems in Sri Lanka. We continue to live in Hope, though time is running out and there is yet no light at the end of the tunnel.

Thank you.

## CHAPTER 13

# THE EYE
# OF THE TIGER

*Do you hear the people sing?*
*Singing the song of angry men?*
*It is the music of a people*
*Who will not be slaves again!*
*When the beating of your heart*
*Echoes the beating of the drums*
*There is a life about to start*
*When tomorrow comes!*

**Les Miserables**

'An eye for and eye and a tooth for a tooth' – so we can all be blind and need dentures.

Secretly, I was disappointed in my father. All old men did was talk. They used words like 'reconciliation' and 'moving forward', 'on-going dialogue'. All this got us nowhere. Since 1956 and Independence Day, we had been systematically bullied as a people and all their 'dialogue' was less than useless.

I had found a new hero and his name was Vellupillai Prabakaran. If you see recent photographs of him you will wonder how this rather dumpy, moustached, middle-aged man mobilised a peaceful people so. You have to imagine him thirty years before when he was young and full of energy. He was an educated man with fire in his belly.

He told the Tamil youth to stand up and be counted. Old men talked and young men (and women) did. He promised freedom; he promised no more oppression and equality for all Tamils. He promised us *Eelam*, our own Tamil lands; after all before the British came, we did have our own kingdoms.

Old men have a lot to lose. They have worked hard for their families; they have jobs and a roof over their heads and children to feed. Young men, particularly if they have no future ahead of them, can be vocal and volatile. That is why students are usually the first to strike or march or join a war. As Cherie Blair famously said of the Palestinians, 'How far must a people have been pushed to react like this?'

In the beginning, the Tigers were very idealistic and made up of passionate young men and women, who really did give everything up for the cause. These were not unemployed ruffians but more like desperate, intelligent graduates, with no future in the new Sinhala, Buddhist, Sri Lanka and nowhere to go.

This original band of Prabakaran supporters were bright, highly motivated, driven individuals. If I was living in Sri Lanka at that time, I can imagine being carried away by the cause. Two things would have stopped me. One was self-preservation, I don't do pain and suffering, and two was my father.

In 1983 they say Sinhala soldiers raped some Tamil girls and that they in turn were attacked by young Tamil men by way of reprisal. This then led to all out violence and civil war. This is when electoral registers were leaked and Tamil homes burned to the ground. People were charred in their cars and dragged out of buses and beaten to death.

Even those who were not supporters of *Eelam* began to wonder if anything was better than this.

Dad had a Tamil friend in London married to a Sinhala lady and his kids were asked in school, 'What is happening in Sri Lanka?' One of them famously answered, 'I think my mother's people are trying to kill my father's people!'

One by one, the youth joined the movement. Initially this seems to have been voluntary and what was peculiar to our conflict was that the number of young women who joined was substantial. Saris were swapped for khaki, hair was cut and family jewellery was melted for the cause.

136

Originally the cause also called for celibacy. Until *Eelam* was achieved, no marriage and no children. It was a bit like becoming a monk, total devotion of body and spirit was demanded, only those with a calling need apply.

Young men and women vanished overnight from school rooms and university classes, from offices and the fields. Heroes were made overnight.

The 'Black Tigers' were also formed and were the most lethal of the group, for even in the beginning 'some were more equal than others'.

If your child disappeared, you kept quiet as if the army found out; the rest of your family would be punished as Tiger sympathisers. A people who loved to gossip were silenced overnight. The Tigers also had the infamy of producing the first ever suicide bombers and they were underestimated at your peril.

The Indians, who came as a peace-keeping force to Sri Lanka, had no idea that they were entering a minefield. They thought that this was an island paradise and a few short weeks of effort would resolve all conflict.

The war lasted from 1983–2009, most of our adult life.

I was in Ceylon with my sister when it started. We were going on holiday from Scotland but my father got word to us to get straight out of Kattunayaka airport and on to any plane, anywhere.

At the airport, ladies sat crying in all their finery. They had literally bedecked themselves and were in their best saris and gold jewellery, leaving in haste, with nothing but what they had on.

My sister was pushing me onto a plane to Singapore and I was resisting, as I thought Dad was over-reacting. The planes were over-booked so mayhem ensued but we eventually got on. Even then we had a bomb scare and my sister and I had an extra glass of wine; better to go out in style and not simpering.

The Sri Lankan press was stifled and reported little. Once in Singapore we tuned into the BBC and were horrified at what we saw. We had to get out of the country to truly grasp what was going on within.

Once home I was incensed and, like my father, wrote letters to the papers, spoke to MPs, gathered petitions for the next decade, to no avail. We wanted economic sanctions against the Sri Lankan government and for the British to cease training Sri Lankan soldiers at Sandhurst.

It would have been easy to become involved in the movement but I had a roof over my head, a loving family, and a place at a British university. I had everything to lose and for all my talk, did not like the principle of violence.

The generations of ministers and doctors in the family had made their mark. It was inconceivable to take another's life.

I clung to my Sri Lankan passport when everyone else had surrendered theirs, including Dad. Sri Lanka did not permit dual citizenship, you had to be one or the other; you had to choose. I thought that once I had graduated, I would go back home, so I held on to mine.

The family used to laugh their heads off when we travelled and I was in a separate queue. A British passport has you flying through customs, or at least it used to. I was a would-be terrorist until proven otherwise. When I was looking for long term employment, I gave up my citizenship. It was causing suspicion about my level of commitment to any job and even I, by then, had to acknowledge that for me the dream of returning soon was over.

Meanwhile Prabakaran was making superhuman progress. Amazing victories were reported and if you consider that Tamils were outnumbered 10:1, it is astonishing that the movement kept the civil war going so long.

Funding came from the 'armchair' politicians abroad and from the locals. The Tigers had their own TV channel and papers, hospitals, training schools for new recruits and so on. In their heyday, they wreaked havoc and created terror in the Sinhala population. They had the government on its knees and even brought down the entire Sri Lankan Air Force. Rajiv Gandhi was first struck by a Sinhala soldier whilst inspecting a parade and subsequently killed by a female Tiger suicide bomber. This had the effect of alienating a number of Indians who had hitherto been sympathetic to the Tamil people. We, a nation famed for our beautiful isle and hospitable nature, were now infamous.

Everyone thought the civil war would last a few years but it dragged on and on and each 'victory' brought reprisals upon the ordinary Tamil people. Casualties rose, civilians fled and recruits started to dwindle. As extreme times demand extreme action, the movement now started to co-opt soldiers, and families lost their sons and daughters but knew full well that their children did not volunteer. Who was there to complain to? If you went to the army they would say you were a sympathiser and if you went to plead with the Tigers they would deny all knowledge or worse still you might be attacked or forced to join too.

One of Dad's friends, in an attempt at 'reconciliation', organised a cricket match between some Tamil students and Sinhala soldiers. He was shot dead by one of his disapproving pupils, who turned out to be a Tiger.

The Tigers had given up everything for the cause and had no compunction about removing jewellery, livestock, land or children from the people they were there to 'save'. After all, was this not the least you could do for the cause?

The people were becoming disillusioned and were hammered on all sides by the government, the Indians and the Tigers. Those that could, got out in droves in planes, on boats and on foot if need be. The old and the poor stayed behind.

Our 'hero' was losing his grip on reality as *Eelam* became elusive and the Tiger movement fragmented and fraught. The world at large had sympathy with the plight of the Tamil people but, particularly after 9/11, not with terrorists. The tide was turning against them.

It took the might of the Chinese army to bring down Prabakaran in the end. The Sri Lankan government made a pact with the Chinese, their new friends, who unlike the British don't worry too much about civilians' rights. Equipped and helped by them, finally victory was achieved and the Tiger movement destroyed.

In one generation, a nation of two million Tamil Lankans was almost halved. Five hundred thousand were dispossessed and a similar number migrated. Forty thousand were killed on the Tamil side and probably double that if you count the total number of deaths on both sides.

My uncle Rajathurai, Ammah's brother, had a tricky time working in the police force at this time. He was posted here, there and everywhere so we never saw much of him. His children were also much younger than us and some born after we left the island, so we did not know them well. His wife was very on the ball and had all her children shipped out as soon as possible.

My aunt Ranee and her family had been told to get out of Sri Lanka. My uncle Ratnarajah had even offered to sort out employment in Africa for them but they refused. They were true nationalists. My aunt is the kind of lady who is more likely to shoot you, than run away. Her husband often worked away from home so she stayed behind and cared for their four children.

Ranee had two daughters and two sons. The boys were much younger than us, so we mixed more with the girls. Her first daughter was a gentle dutiful soul and most unlike her. Her second daughter was spirited and wilful, like her mother.

This girl was called Thusha and she was at school when civil war broke out. She was a straight 'A' student and wanted to be a doctor. She studied hard but whenever she came back from classes some army official would tease her or pull her bag or say something offensive.

One day she did not come home from school. Ranee did not worry at first, thinking she was at a friend's or late with her studies. My uncle was away and the other children had to be looked after, so my aunt could not go far to look for Thusha. She also had to be careful who she spoke to about her missing daughter.

Two days passed and by now my aunt had travelled everywhere looking for my cousin. She went to the school, to Thusha's friends' houses, her usual haunts but the girl had vanished. A young man, seeing the distraught mother, told her what she had dreaded and secretly suspected – that Thusha had gone to train at the Tiger camp.

She was not satisfied with this and forced the boy to take her. These places were tucked in the jungle in secret locations and hard to access. Going there was often a one-way trip, unless you were invited or had come to join the movement.

Ranee was only permitted as far as the entrance gate. She clung to the gates for two days wailing, 'Thusha, Thusha *pillai*, come back.'

She made such a racket that, eventually, Thusha was forced to come out and silence her. She told her mother that there was no point living as they did. There was no future for any of them being bullied and subjugated as Tamils, she was fighting for a better life for them all, in *Eelam*. She told her mother to go away. Once you became a Tamil Tiger you no longer had a mother, father, or personal relationships. These things were no longer important, for the cause was all that mattered.

My aunt never told me this story; I found it out from someone else twenty years later. She is a proud lady and she used to pretend that she supported Thusha, she behaved as if she was honoured to have a Tiger in the family. We thought she was a bit irresponsible as a mother, but we really had no idea that these tales were to save face. She was destroyed by her loss but she was not going to show it.

I saw a Tiger pamphlet once and there was my cousin in full military attire. She looked fearsome and magnificent, as she had climbed quite high in the organisation. What had become of the girl who loved to act in plays, listen to music and dance wildly?

My aunt went home and continued life with her remaining three children.

One day an Indian army officer came down her drive and said, 'Madam we have to take your furniture, it is requisitioned for the Indian army.'

He was surprised to find her reply in English, 'You go to hell. You soldiers have taken our food and taken our land and our children, you will not take any more from me.'

The poor soldier did not really understand how he had managed to do all of that but she looked fearsome, so he turned back and went looking for easier pickings.

If a Tigress dies, the movement said they would send a messenger to leave a rose on the mother's doorstep, and then the family would know. My cousin is dead. We all know it, but Ranee pretends it isn't so, for no one has sent her a rose. We know the rose will never come; it is not possible, for the messengers are dead also.

My aunt and her family migrated to India as their connections came to haunt them and they feared for their other children. Her remaining three children then migrated further afield for education. My uncle later developed a brain tumour and required surgery. This was done at a private hospital in India and he suffered complications of surgery which left him blind and brain damaged.

Ranee the beauty queen of our family, who defying everyone, entered and won the contest dressed in Sinhala national costume, now lives in a foreign country, with none of her children or relatives around her, caring for her disabled husband.

The television flashes pictures of my hero Prabakaran. A family photograph with his handsome son. I think, 'You lied to us. You got married. You had a child and see what happened to that poor child, you became corrupt and *Eelam* never came.'

Everyone should be made to go to Passchendaele. It should become a compulsory part of the school curriculum. When I went I was initially quite sanguine about it. Personally I go to Belgium for the chocolate but it is part of the tour, so you go.

I have nothing to do with the First or even the Second World War. The only memory we have is a story my father tells us, of seeing African Americans for the first time. Dad must have felt right at home with them. He said they were very jolly chaps and used to throw sweets at the kids. None of my family were much involved in these wars, apart from some of the Handys who were evacuated from Malaysia and came to stay in Guru Vasa for a while.

In Passchendaele you see row upon row of crosses. White against the blue skyline and many with the inscription,

'Known only to God.'

The human carnage is over whelming. When will we ever learn? War is man's inhumanity to man, and civil war, when brother fights brother, is particularly vicious.

Everyone is damaged, those who die, the 'victorious' who have lost a piece of humanity and those who watch and survive like me.

*There's a grief that can't be spoken.*
*There's a pain goes on and on*
*Empty chairs at empty tables*
*Now my friends are dead and gone ...*

*Here they talked of revolution*
*Here it was they lit the flame*
*Here they sang about tomorrow*
*But tomorrow never came.*

*Oh my friends, my friends forgive me*
*That I live and you are gone*
*There's a grief that can't be spoken*
*There's a pain goes on and on.*

Les 'Miserables'

CHAPTER 14

# A NARROW
# ESCAPE

All Iyah and Appammah wanted was their children and grandchildren about them, but at one time five children lived in five continents.

First, Daniel went to America, but this was really due to his chosen speciality of sociology, rather than due to Ceylon politics. My father got stuck in Britain having been blacklisted by the government and my Aunts Manie and Chandra left for Zambia and Nigeria and then on to Australia. Only my *Chithappah* Balan, remained with them.

We had all been educated in English, a language widely spoken in the world but the Government, keen to shake off its colonial past, decided that from hence forth all should speak, read and write in Sinhala. Many of my cousins were at the point of sitting university entrance exams so this abrupt switch was quite a trial. My uncle Kanagarajah always keen to rise to new challenges employed a Sinhala gentleman who used to arrive at their house on a bicycle and the whole family would gather to learn.

After a few months the children grew restless and my uncle had the horrible suspicion that this was just the tip of the iceberg in terms of getting his children into university. 'Standardisation' was then also imposed and meant that as the Tamils were only ten per cent of the population, they would only be given ten per cent of the university places. Even this meagre number was not policed, so in short if you were Tamil in the new Sri Lanka, you were less likely to get a place at university or any institution of higher education.

This predictably caused a lot of youth unrest and rioting in those who were not Sinhala or Buddhist and both my male cousins came under suspicion as young trouble makers, though they had done nothing.

It could be argued that the British left a time bomb, as the industrious Tamils, who were very much a minority, had many of the prestigious posts in government and the civil service and so were left in charge of the majority. In the UK, when Gordon Brown was PM, I overheard many disgruntled English folk say, why should a Scotsman be leading us? Just imagine how the English majority would feel if half of Parliament was Scottish too. Many of the best schools were in the north of the island, as its soil was dry and not as fertile as the south, so education was the way forward for these peoples rather than agriculture. They became a hyper-educated nation.

My uncles felt that their sons and daughters were in danger and would never amount to anything in their own country. Simply learning Sinhala was not enough. As engineers, they both got posts easily in Africa where mining and building were booming. They were offered houses with gardens, cars, drivers and housekeepers, good schools for their children and salaries that would enable them to send their offspring to any university in the world.

Like many of our middle-class intelligentsia, (Tamil/Sinhala and Burgher alike), they left. Bit by bit the country lost a lot of its brain power. Those who were less skilled, less moneyed or more nationalistic remained, forming a worrying cohort.

One of my male cousins was very playful and a great cricketer. He rapidly settled into the good life in Africa and studying was not a favourite preoccupation. He was a sociable and popular chap and forever out with his friends or partying away. My uncle packed him off to the UK to get him away from a life of opulent indolence.

When he arrived we were euphoric, though he was less so. At last we had a relative who was not one of the five of us. My parents treated him like an extra child and were very mindful of his loneliness. He would come to us for Christmas and various holidays and enjoy Ammah's cooking instead of the boiled offerings at university.

He describes arriving in Preston to study, knowing not one soul. The last piece of advice given by his father was, 'Do not talk to any Sri Lankans and make new British friends.' My cousin used to feel tearful every day but my uncle clearly knew what he was doing, as away from all the African distractions he studied, made good and became highly successful, being part of the IT boom.

In contrast I sit here now worrying about the possibility of my daughter going to Glasgow, instead of Edinburgh University; I need to see her and what she is up to! My parents' generation made harsh choices as they were cornered; there was no time for tears.

My father's younger brother Balan was the last to remain. He was an accountant and had already done a bit of trouble shooting and was offered various posts in Australia. He always came back to Sri Lanka until one day looters came down his street. His Sinhala neighbours warned him and the whole family jumped over the wall and hid in a neighbour's toilet. If I was ever forced to go in hiding, this would definitely be the place for me; I could cope without most things but not sanitation.

The looters had electoral registers and our long, unpronounceable Tamil names were an easy give away. Tamils also tend to have sharper features than Sinhalese and are generally easily picked out.

Mrs Manikam had saved them, for the name Sanders caused confusion. The looters banged on the Sinhalese neighbour's door and my cousins had to put their hands over their mouths and try to keep quiet, as their 'Samaritan' insisted that the Sanders' were Sinhala.

The neighbours put themselves at great risk and had they been found to be harbouring Tamils, would no doubt have been killed off too as sympathisers. After a few days in the toilet my uncle decided that they had to go back home, it was not fair to put others in danger on their behalf. Their house had been looted and anything the thugs could not take was broken. My cousins wept at the remnants of their treasured piano and my little 'Baby Sanders' cousin at the loss of Teddy.

Once again friends and neighbours came to the rescue and lent pots and pans, bits of furniture and they became squatters in their own house. They tried to keep cheerful and think of it as a camping expedition, all the damage was bad enough but the terror of looters returning was never far away.

My uncle tried to keep things normal and returned to work whilst also trying to secure visas and tickets to get out. My cousins even went on the bus to school as normal; there was simply nothing else for it.

145

Now 'Baby Sanders' was the bravest of little girls and quite in a mood about it all. The loss of Teddy was particularly unbearable and one day on the bus she saw him in another girl's arms. She would have almost certainly attacked this little girl and got her precious back, if not for the restraining arms of my aunt Susila. This one act would have given the game away completely.

Whilst they were living quietly, the Sri Lankan news failed to represent the truth but the BBC broadcast riots, looting and the burning of Tamils. Journalists who dared to publish what was real were in grave danger. The whole family lived in terror until they got on the plane to Australia and never looked back. They are not as sentimental as me and my siblings about Sri Lanka, because they suffered much.

So there we all were, in Africa, America, Australia and Europe but not in Asia. After generations of Sanders and Manikams and whatever else we were thousands of years before that, we were gone.

There is a wonderful expression which is 'What doesn't kill you, makes you stronger.' My Sanders cousins, my siblings and I had a very messy start; our education was all over the place. I think my sister holds the record for eight schools in total. Our friends came and went and our childhood was quite disrupted. We were the lucky ones however, as we got away. We did not lose family members or see things a child should never see. We were not tortured. We were not shot at.

I think our children take much for granted and because they were not backed into a corner the way we were, I am not sure how they will turn out. They are like plants too long in the green house. My father used to always tell me when I faced any adversity, 'Stand up and stop crying. Sanders girls don't cry, ever.'

There is always a trade-off however, as we know exactly who we are and where we came from. I think these children will have a period of confusion ahead as they work out their Ceylonese/Scottish/whatever else roots they have, and try to clear a path for themselves. I suppose that is partly why I am committing our history to paper.

# CHAPTER 15

# DOES YOUR MOTHER KNOW?

Our mother would tell the three of us all the time that we were the cleverest, best looking, most talented children in the world. It had to be true, because mothers are not supposed to tell lies and we believed her completely.

This self-assurance helped us greatly. When my brother was repeatedly bullied at school because of his colour, by boys often twice his age, he never backed down. If I tried to help him he would tell me to keep out of it or I would make things worse for him.

When half the class never spoke to me or my sister because we were foreign, we imagined ourselves to be too superior to mix with the likes of them. We were plants lucky enough to be given such a good start that no wind would uproot us.

In my last years at school, I finally found my best friend. Her name was Michele which means 'Gift of God'. She was called this because she had a hole in her heart but she and I could walk for miles. There was no topic that we could not discuss with each other and although these days I do not call her as much as I should, she still has the capacity to understand things from a unique viewpoint. She was and is a girl of independent thought and action. In many ways we were total opposites, as I am so much a product of my environment.

There was also a boy, a blonde haired, blue eyed boy called Jonathan. At one point, he was the only person in school who could run faster than me. Jonathan and Michele were unique in the seventies because they were 'colour blind'. I grew up in a much more racist world, one in which you could have easily been made to feel inferior and where there were virtually no other fellow Asians where we lived in Scotland.

Jonathan and I lost touch a few years after I left school but if I met him again I would shake his hand and say thanks for dancing with me when no one else would and saving me from the humiliation of repeated waltzes with the teacher. Thanks for standing for hours and helping me sign my petitions and for making me feel more like a girl than a boy and for inviting me to meet your lovely family, as no other boy in that era ever did. I heard that he has settled down, that he found girl and is married now. I hope all his dreams came true. She is a Sinhalese girl, who is a friend of a friend.

My parents were forward thinking for their day and would discuss with us not only topics relating to our education and morals but also their concerns about how we would meet and marry someone living isolated from our own people in Scotland.

My sister was born with a stethoscope, so it was no surprise that she went to medical school. This was the first time that she was on a level playing field and not playing catch up with her education. In some ways she was very like Harriet; jolly and fun to be with and, like Harriet, she had no guile, always believing the best of people. The university was much more cosmopolitan than school, and once there, she had a number of friends of varied nationality.

Her female friends ranged from a ballet dancer, who looked like Elizabeth Taylor and seemed to be doing medicine just for fun, to those so passionate about work, that they are currently some of the leading physicians in their speciality in the UK.

Of the boys who were would be suitors, one was an eccentric genius, a South African who had far too much money for his own good and a hilarious, unscrupulous lad, who would probably have been struck off by now.

The medical student I remember most was probably the best looking chap I have ever seen in flesh and blood. He was a gentle soul who had many female admirers and a challenging moral outlook to match. Though he was very keen on her, even she knew that the outcome was unlikely to be good. My sister threw herself back into her studies, as this was something she could be sure of.

My brother and I found all of this most amusing. In the end she met my current brother-in-law. He went in hot pursuit of her and she finally saw the light. My brother-in-law seemed to come as part of a package, in that he had four close friends who never left his side. When they came home for dinner, we would all have quite a riot and play music and talk till the early hours. They were all very fond of my sister and always arrived to see her with a large bunch of flowers, frequently resembling those that bloomed on the round-about near her home.

My sister was ever conscious of her 'right-hand man role' and knew that whatever she did set the tone for her siblings. It is hard being the eldest child as parents often make their mistakes here and correct them by the time other children come to face the same issues.

When she got straight As, my brother would say, 'What a pain, now the parents will expect this of us too.' I never really got that bit and when my mother kept asking, 'What do you want to do *pillai?*' the answer was easy: 'Nothing.'

My parents, in some ways, did us no favours. Their love was selfless and seamless; it flowed like the *Mahaweli Ganga* (famous Sri Lankan river) into the deep Indian Ocean. They were incomplete without the other and we thought this was quite normal. We had no idea of 'modern love' which required much more bartering and calculating.

I was intrinsically the most cautious and measured out of the three, so that made me less vulnerable. I still recall my brother and sister singing and dancing wildly to a song called 'I Surrender', the general gist of which is that you would do anything, give anything, and abandon yourself entirely for love. I thought it a particularly foolish and dangerous viewpoint.

One of my cousins used to write in every autograph book, 'Never fall in love because it's a terrible fall.' That's exactly right. In fact never fall at all if you can help it, or you may break something. Love can come when you least expect it. It may not flow from the most obvious sources and if you are really unlucky, it may not come at all.

The whole marriage thing really bothered my parents and they really did not know what to do. If we had been in Ceylon, we would have mixed in the right circles and met and married someone suitable, like our aunts and uncles had done. The task required of relatives and well-meaning friends was to introduce you to the right sort of person, but this was not going to be possible for us in Scotland.

Meanwhile times were changing and my brother, being much younger than both of us, more outgoing and a boy, had a bevy of girls after him. He became Scottish Cross-Country Schools' Champion and used to train in the university grounds. I would love to go and see him and time his runs. Girls would regularly stare at me and eventually one would ask, 'Are you Dave's girlfriend?' to which I smiled and answered, 'Yes.'

Ever a boy to make as much trouble for himself as he could, he brought home an Egyptian Muslim girl. We all had grave concerns about this and her family were the most unfortunate type of Muslims. They were moderate Muslims, who are in fact the majority, locked in a lose-lose situation due to the vocal extremists. The fundamentalists detested this group and non-Muslims presumed they were fundamentalists. Her parents were both doctors and bizarrely, Appah and her dad had a secretary who worked for both at different times. The Arabic nations are some of the most hospitable in the world and her parents were great fun to be with and fabulous hosts.

Once in medical school, my brother followed the same path as Dad did many years before; he did no work and tried his hardest to get thrown out. He was badly behaved and rude to anyone he did not like, so I used to pretend that I was not closely related to him.

I hated studying but found a good group of friends at university. I went to various discos and gigs with this group and frequently felt that I seemed to be being followed by a boy. The same chap would also get on and off the bus when I went home. I used to tell him a load of rubbish to try to get rid of him. I think my first line was 'I'm a Sunday school teacher (true) and I don't drink (lie).' In short, don't think you are going to get me drunk and have your wicked way with me.

In my third year he ended up sitting next to me and I was struggling to remember all the lies I had told. He was tagging our group because he knew he was later to join our year. He wore me down so I took him home in the end.

'*Chi chi chi*', my mother said. 'An Indian, a vegetarian and now you tell me an asthmatic.'

'Appah, tell her no.'

To this my father's response was, 'Whatever you want daught.'

What I wanted was a Ceylonese Christian but that simply was not going to happen. Though bright, caring and multi-talented, my choice brought with it racial and dietary challenges. He was of Indian origin, vegetarian and a non-Christian. Having spent much of life saying,

'No! I'm not Indian', this was an interesting predicament to be in.

No one ever asked me to become vegetarian but if you marry someone and always want you own way, you are heading down an unhappy path. If you give in on all matters the same is true also. Contentment lies in working out what matters for each of you and what can be compromised. For a girl whose favourite food was lump rice and Ammah's mutton curry, who barely touched, never mind ate green things, this was a brave new world.

What I would not compromise on was religion. I wanted a Christian wedding and for my children to be baptised. My father was a clever man; he did not treat each of his children in the same way. He would have never said to my other siblings, 'Whatever you want.' He worked out the pros and cons of each child and changed his stance accordingly.

My mother woke up from her sleep and became very vocal.

What was I thinking of? The Indians were quite a patriarchal society, unlike us, how would I stomach that?

Of all her children, I was the most nationalistic; the last one she would have thought would do this.

'Vegetarians. What do you feed them?'

'I don't care if you love me or hate me. I have to tell you all of this and make you think.'

I thought that she was fabulous. I was her only concern. She did not want me to be unhappy. It was never about other people or what they might say.

'Sanders is a loser, see how those children are running wild.'

My mother forced me to think, and that was a good thing but the answer was still the same. Back in Mumbai my would-be extended family gathered to hear the news of our marriage and wept. No one had ever married outside their caste and class. A total foreigner, what next?

I did not want a big wedding but the other side did. So the negotiations started, what sort of food, what sort of clothing, where, when, how, auspicious days, a concept we do not have as Christians.

We could have booked a Thomson's wedding and dumped them all but what is that saying? None of you are important, only we matter. These early discussions are vital for setting the pace of the married life to come.

My intended's gentle father said to Appah, 'The prospect of animals being

151

slaughtered for my son's marriage saddens me so.'

Appah said, 'The prospect of my family and friends travelling for miles to chew on carrots saddens me so.'

The Gujaratis from India have a tradition whereby, before the wedding, the groom's family come to the bride's house laden with saris and jewellery. I thought this tradition should definitely be adhered to. My *Chithappah* Balan and *Chinammah* Susila came for my wedding and, when confronted with theses boxes of jewels, were quite bemused. Appah was having one of his 'can't be bothered talking' days and, to compensate for the silences, my uncle was charming.

On the day of the wedding my in-laws were quite confused as they wondered why the father was sitting (Balan), whilst the quiet, dark guy was walking me down the aisle of the church.

We had a very large wedding, which I am sure nearly bankrupted my father. Both parties wanted to pay but he insisted, as this was our tradition. At the reception following the ceremony there was a vegetarian meal and jazz music. I had Indian, Lankan and Scottish guests and likewise my bridesmaids, pageboys and flower girls were of each nationality.

Michele was a flaxen beauty in blue and my cousin proved to be so irresistible to my brother's friends, that we were cautious about where we seated her and reminded them that she was definitely going back to Australia. At the end of the wedding day Appah and Michele went to the chip shop as 'carrots' were not enough.

My parents' concerns were well-founded and I would be lying if I say marrying a foreigner is easy. My main concern about marrying a European was the divorce rate. We were not brought up to have several boyfriends and give of ourselves freely. We were taught to believe ourselves precious and to value our emotions and our bodies.

If you went out with Tom as he was bright and Dick for his physical attributes, by the time you got to Harry, even if he is the right man you have spent yourself. No one gets everything and in the words of Abba 'take it easy, take it easy, take it nice and slow, does your mother know?'

If someone truly loves you, they will not pressure you into doing something you do not want. Nothing wrong with telling mother; in most cases she has your best interest at heart.

My generation of women are failing their sons and daughters. Is it really satisfactory to let a series of women and men come and go in your life? Is this really what we want? Through the centuries women, not men, have been the spiritual compass. What are we saying to our children? What about your mental investment, is this not a hidden cost? Life is not fair and men and women are not the same, for women are often left with the consequences of this approach to relationships.

I have seen many young ladies in my professional life who have been almost bullied into sexual relationships for fear of being thought a prude. They do not stand up for themselves and their mothers say, 'What can we do?' which is in my opinion, especially when these girls are young teenagers living with them, unacceptable. Is a very young girl capable of informed consent?

We have to all stop worshipping at the gym and trying to keep eternally young with botox and fillers. This is a battle that can never be won and if a bit more time was spent instead developing the spirit rather than the body, we are much more likely to achieve well-being. You could argue that a Christian would say that but even the British Medical Journal had to admit in a recent study that people with a faith, any sort of faith, fared better when unwell and dying than those without.

The world is now jeans, pop music and McDonald's all over but in the past our assumption was that Asian men were a safer bet than their European counter parts and more family-orientated. They can, however also be deeply chauvinistic, insular and much less fun.

There is a bit of luck involved in these choices; even the best person can make a mistake and sometimes, however much you think you know someone, a few years of co-habiting prove you wrong. My husband was one of those gentlemanly intellectuals, a quiet hero, who knew what he would and would not do. We wove our own path and as it was an untrodden one, we made it up as we went along.

As Mumbai has not the troubles of Sri Lanka, we go there as often as we can and my extended family has showered our children with love and affection. It is a place bursting with life and energy and when you visit, you feel it too.

I do not know what our children will do. We can only equip them with the tools and a sense of self-worth and value. They must work out each for themselves what matters and what can be conceded. I do hope though that they do not compromise on their belief in God, not for my sake but because in my darkest times it has been for me, and many before me, our salvation.

Iyah's and Appammah's grandchildren could easily open their own branch of the United Nations. In our fold we have Americans, Malaysians, Indians, Egyptians and Australians.

My brother has one son. He was born on 9/11 and is half Egyptian Muslim and half Ceylon Tamil. When he grows up I will buy him robust walking shoes, as he is a boy who should definitely avoid air travel.

I am not sure what my Iyah would have made of all of this. His mind was less flexible than my father's, so I suspect he would have been disappointed. It takes a unique sort of person to cross the bridge to foreign waters. It is not an easy choice to make and had our systems not disintegrated, I suspect that I would have remained deeply traditional and never bothered.

Perhaps we all pay in the end, as when you get older you often revert back to familiar childhood things, eating with your hands, waiting desperately until you find a bidet, inadvertently calling someone 'a bugger' at a meeting. This is when those who have come from the same origins will win. No explanations are needed, for so much you could not even put into words is shared.

I always put my career second. It was a great sacrifice as you can tell. For me my greatest role was to provide a loving home for my family. I laugh my head off when I read, 'Women failing to achieve top posts in whatever', they are not failing, many of them just don't want it.

You simply can't have it all, unless you abandon your family and your children this is just not possible. It is bad enough when men do it.

There is a fabulous book by a chap called Steven Covey and he says, 'Let's start with your funeral.' I think it is great advice, that way you can work backwards at what counts for you. I never wanted 'and she wrote some fantastic papers'; 'Baked great cake, gave a lot of love to family and friends' is good enough for me.

If I wasn't brought up to Christian ways I think the idea of monogamy would be a challenge. Three husbands for each phase of life would be adequate. One for fun in youth, the current one for my middle age and as Appah used to say to Ammah, 'If you give me trouble, a trade in', for the last phase of life.

I tell my daughter, 'Your brother will be the love of your life', and she laughs. 'It's true, you will most likely know him the longest. Parents, children and even husbands may come and go, but you will only have one brother.'

He is very kind to her. She has him well trained and he brings her coffee in bed. I tell her, 'Look after him. Don't be just a taker, be a giver too.'

She says, 'Mum, who do you think does all the nerd's homework?'

CHAPTER 16

# RETURN TO PARADISE

Once my father had established that he was not returning long term to Sri Lanka, and new governments came and went, he got the all clear to return. If you were 'out' with one government you were 'in' with another, so that's how it worked.

He had lost all he had left behind and had to start again in his forties in Britain, so we had a modest home and only one income for five. He never seemed to mind that in a way I would have, as we were all safe and together. Our little semi-detached house was a cheerful place. Our neighbours, the Macdonalds, were 'attached to us' and would pop in and out. Various friends came and went, music would play, there were endless cooking sessions and fighting children were ever present creating the background noise.

There were a few trips to Sri Lanka but always in ones or twos as we could not afford to go all together. The parents were also cautious because some Sri Lankans who were deemed traitors had their passports confiscated at Kattunayaka airport. Though my father had paid back every penny of his scholarship money he was viewed as a 'fugitive'.

My sister and I went once and decided we were bringing back tropical fish for our brother, fruits for Dad and all of Ammah's jewellery. Our relatives advised that this was not possible and some of this required a permit, so we carried a can with a little water and the fish were well concealed within. We buried the fruits in our suitcases and wore all of Ammah's jewels. Ah, the glorious days before scans. Then, people did not suspect little girls of smuggling.

All the fish made it but later died, as we did not have a proper tank or environment to look after them and mistakenly believed they would do fine in a bowl. We have some epic pictures of the brother screaming and crying, again, and the poor little fish floating on the top of his glass orb; maybe not such a great gift after all.

My parents went back to see Iyah and Appammah too. My father felt that he had failed them, as he was not there to look after them in their old age.

In 1983, when the riots broke out, this all came to a halt. It was just not a safe place to go and by then Iyah, thankfully, had passed away and was not there to see the mess. Appammah was globetrotting, exploring the homes of her far flung offspring and the pull to return was less.

My father loved his country so and mourned its loss. His work, though enjoyable, was very stressful and a number of early migrants who were fortunate enough to achieve success had the same experience. Now systems are more transparent and 'diversity' is embraced. Then you had to work at two hundred percent to get anywhere. He had little time for hobbies and was not physically at his best.

I once asked my dad why he never came swimming with us and he said, 'After you have swum and fished in the Indian Ocean, splashing around four concrete walls or artificial ponds is unattractive.' He never went fishing in the UK either, which was a great shame as he used to find it a calming, spiritual experience.

There were also financial strains, as he alone funded all aspects of our life and as all three of us went to university and spent many years there, not earning. This went on and on. He practically set off fireworks when my sister graduated and there was one less dependent. She was ever generous and suddenly we were having meals out and able to holiday where we liked and not just at friends' homes. This was the greatest luxury of all.

My father always seemed calm to me. We all saw explosions of temper if he was crossed, but whoever it was annoying him, usually had it coming. Of course it was never me. On reflection he internalised a lot. Like my grandfather he would have a quiet spell in the morning and no one was allowed to talk to him whilst he contemplated his day, and whatever else was bothering him.

During this hour he would consume several cups of coffee and cigarettes and then set off to battle, that being work.

The age of the manager was dawning and he was not for it. Suddenly he had no idea how many beds he had and patients unknown to him would occupy them. Continuity of care was threatened as he ceased to have sole responsibility for his patients and 'efficiency' savings were all the rage.

At this point my brother's challenging behaviour rose to new dizzy heights and father and son were like two bulls in a pen. I think it is often like this, it has to be, as otherwise the invariable parting would be unbearable. When he left home my father gave him a Bible and wrote in it, 'Son, the answers are all right here.'

As it was, I was delighted when my brother left home. I had the undivided attention of my parents for the first time in my life and had to be prised away from them like a limpet. Because I did not have a standard childhood, I valued being with them. I enjoyed a good social life at university and all the comforts of a loving home. I am sure my parents would have had little purpose in life without me.

In the 1990s, the Sri Lankan problem grew and grew and we became more isolated from our fellow countrymen because of our views. Dad's work became more stressful, my uncle Daniel died suddenly and both my aunts and my grandmother fell ill simultaneously.

My brother had organised a short holiday for my parents to cheer them up. I was lying on the couch after a particularly satisfying Sunday lunch and watching *How Green Was My Valley* with Dad. Ammah was cleaning up; she loved to do this all by herself and spoil me. I wouldn't have dreamed of interfering with her vocation. Appah was telling me that David had organised the Grand National for him to attend and, having never quite lost his love for horse racing and gambling, he looked forward to going. They were over stretched at work, so he planned to drive down after a full day at the hospital.

Once at the Grand National the place was heaving with humanity and someone tried to grab my mother's bag and failed but stole my father's wallet. He was clearly not in good form and tackled the thief.

He then told my brother, 'Take me to hospital; I think I am having a stroke.'

'Seriously not a funny joke Dad', was my brother's curt reply.

The great thing about being a doctor was that, as they sped along to hospital, Dad could work out exactly which anatomical area of the brain was getting damaged.

A few hours later he lost consciousness. We were all called to his bedside and my sister was pregnant with Gideon, so we had a ready replacement if Dad was planning to exit. We called the baby Gideon because he rotated a lot in utero, so was probably giddy. The baby was especially responsive to music.

Appah then started to fit, as he had suffered a bleed rather than a clot into his brain and this caused cerebral irritation. After this we heard 'the death rattle' or cheyne-stokes breathing, as it is called in the trade.

My sister's husband, being a Sri Lankan, took charge and knew what to do, so we stood around the hospital bed, said our prayers and prepared for the worst. My mother was in another world, being quite unrealistic and saying things like,

'No, darling, you are not going. Who will wind my watch, who will talk to me and look after me?'

She was quite able to 'wind her watch' and look after herself, so this really was nonsense. She kept going on and on, and was sure to nag him out of his coma.

'Stop it Mummy, this is it, brace yourself', I told her.

'Don't talk rubbish. This is not it. He is not going to leave me', she replied firmly.

My father's stroke was right sided and quite dense. When he was really bad, I swore I would not leave his side. As it was thought that he was going to die, we were given a side room and Ammah and I sat with him. There were only chairs available and sleep, especially with all the weird noises he was making, was near impossible.

My siblings and I had all had the pleasure of working a hundred hours a week, before this was made illegal, so I was disappointed when I only lasted two days. It was not just the fatigue; I seemed to be having some sort of melt down. After that my siblings and I took it in turn to attend him.

My fluffy 'lightweight' mother remained at my father's side for six weeks. She sat the whole time in a chair and only left him to toilet and once a week to go to the chapel and harass God instead.

It is hard to delude yourself when you are a doctor and death is staring you in the face, but relatives often do this.

In consultation with my siblings 'not for 222' (do not resuscitate) was written on my father's notes. When he woke up a few days later, he said, 'Who put that in my notes?' Being the most helpful of his three children I told him immediately, 'It wasn't me, Dad. I did not speak to the doctor, Rosh and David did.'

I later asked him, ever insightful as I am, 'Would you rather be dead?'

'No. I am alive for a reason and I will get better.'

In his sleep, my father returned to Ceylon and spoke in the most traditional high powered Tamil, so much so that we could not understand him. He generally always spoke to us in English and all we knew were a few Tamil words for 'idiot' and 'fool', so this was quite strange.

In the 1990s if you had a stroke, doctors walked past your bed embarrassed because there was little they could do. The cheerful, ever optimistic physiotherapists and nurses kept our spirits up and Appah, ever determined, established his own rehab programme once home.

I thought vanity had overwhelmed him when he mirrored his garage, till I realised he was watching his gait. He had a bike, tennis balls and various bits and bobs for training. He did this every day and occasionally my sister and I would join him to break the monotony of this routine.

Life is scary. One day you are a big man strutting around the corridors of the hospital with your retinue behind you, the next you are a patient and learning how to walk and eat.

My father also tried to keep his mind sharp by doing crosswords and watching programmes that facilitated this. He loved Scrabble and would never pass up the opportunity to challenge us. David was very keen for a game when he came to visit and was sorely disappointed when he lost.

'Son, the thing is, I have lost a number of neurones it's true, but since I had considerably more than you to start with, you still have no chance of winning!'

In anyone's life there will always be times of darkness but sooner or later the light will come. The light was our first child Danny. Well, he was not actually mine, he was technically my sister's but that was irrelevant to me. We weren't far off the mark thinking of him as a replacement as he looked just like Dad and had those enormous Handy eyes. He and Appah were great companions from day one and learned to walk together. We changed our mind about calling him Gideon; he would have been teased relentlessly at school.

Thankfully Appah had not lost any vision after his stroke but however hard he tried to get better, it became apparent that if he returned to work he would not be able to carry out all his duties. He did not want to go back substandard and a burden to colleagues. Mentally he was all there, which was miraculous but he could not walk fast. Stairs had become a big challenge and his powerful right arm, once used for boxing, fishing and basketball was now spastic and weak. He decided to retire.

On the plus side, I had his undivided attention and for the next thirteen years we celebrated everything. He even travelled abroad again, including to Sri Lanka with my brother and his wife, and saw the birth of five grandchildren.

In the year 2000, my parents had been married forty years and whilst we were planning secret parties, he had organised for us all to celebrate in Disney World. I wondered if he was a much bigger baby than any of us thought but all he wanted was to see his grandchildren's faces when confronted by Mickey and Pluto. This was their kids' paradise and my parents, ever selfless, had the greatest pleasure from their pleasure.

As the years passed and he became frailer and his limbs more unyielding in spite of all he did, it became obvious that they had to move. He was not keen to become a 'satellite' to his daughters and burden them but we encouraged him to come to Edinburgh. Childcare was exorbitant, who wouldn't pass up free help! David remained in England, so being close to him and so far from their friends and both daughters was a less attractive proposition.

I was set the unenviable task of finding them a new home. The property boom was well on its way and people played games and expected fifty percent above the asking price for their homes. It was soul destroying, the cycle of excitement, offer and rejection. Eventually I would look people in the face and say, 'My father is unwell and trying to move near me. This is all he can afford, is it good enough? He hasn't got time or money to waste.'

It's amazing how honest people are if you say that. I might try it even if it isn't true. I finally found a smart, small flat near us, with a balcony.

'Wonderful. I see you have discovered the waiting room to God,' was the sarcastic observation, for as he stepped out, he faced a sea of balconies, with elderly people seated out.

'If all the grandchildren come and jump about as they do, what will these people say?' Ammah complained.

So I went in a huff for a few weeks to see if he could do better, clearly my parents had no idea. He then found a bungalow on the internet and asked me to go and see it. The seller thought I was jesting when I said, 'He can't be bothered driving to see it but if you accept my offer, he will regard it as binding.'

So, another phase when we were all near each other ensued and the grandchildren flourished with all the love and attention given. My parents joined our local church and the support and welcome was heart-warming. My husband, who had never attended before and was not Christian, helped my father to go to church each week. It is hard to make friends again when you are old; the church was a vital link with their new community.

In 2005 Appah felt things seemed to have gone quiet in Lanka and as I had been keen to visit for many years he felt I should seize the opportunity. I had not set foot on my island for twelve years.

'What do I do when I get there Dad?'

'Take a picture of the cycus tree.'

'Yes. I'll take lots of pictures of all of it, to show our children. I'll visit Iyah's grave. What shall I tell him?'

'Tell him I'll be seeing him real soon.'

'Very funny dad. You are hilarious!'

So my husband and I went with our children, aged ten and seven. They loved the beaches and the heat, the sun, the food and the beauty of the country. They thought the people kind and friendly. We did the usual tourist things and the elephants at Yalla were, predictably, their favourite thing. They are beautiful gentle beasts and when they emerge en masse from the water, it is a spiritual experience. They were here before us and once ruled this kingdom.

I was impatient to take the plane to Jaffna. On the approach, it all changed. From the air we saw once beautiful homes, with their tops blown off. I was told to stop filming. There were soldiers everywhere on arrival and guns very apparent. My son was very unimpressed when his Gameboy was dismantled in case it was an explosive device. The children were frightened.

Some young men met us once in the city, they were quite persistent and I was at pains to explain, in my broken Tamil, that we had a driver coming. My husband was being particularly irritating and kept saying, 'We are Indian,' for he realised that these were Tigers looking for 'a donation' for their cause.

We got a room in a guest house in Nallur minutes from my beloved Guru Vasa. I could not wait and we flung our bags and made haste. The driver was an imbecile who just dumped us in some random place and claimed we had arrived. Did this man think I was a foolish tourist he could swindle?

I had forgotten the harsh Jaffna sun and was getting in a bit of a state and my husband advised that we take a look around. In the midst of this ruin and rubble, squatters had settled in a makeshift shed and were watching on bemused. They looked poor abandoned creatures. There was no foliage at all to be seen and certainly no cycus tree.

I was getting hotter and hotter and angrier. I had not come this long way to be messed about. Then I saw it; a few pieces of Italian tile, unique to Guru Vasa. The remnants of the arch that led to Iyah's office, now heralded an empty space. I headed for the squatters in my rage and shouted, 'You are in my house. My grandfather lived here. You are in my house.'

The squatter said to his son,

'Get madam a *Vimto* from the *kaddia* across the street. She is very upset.'

'Yes madam, we knew your grandfather, he was a fine man. He would not have minded; we have nowhere to go.'

Oddly all that was left standing tall was the old outhouse. Our legacy was now the toilet. The army had bombed Guru Vasa, for the lands around it were so vast and they felt Tigers may be hiding there. This way they could see clearly and they took up occupation of Manie Marmie's house next door, which was strategically situated by the Kattcheri junction.

Across the street bizarrely the *kaddai* was fully intact as it used to be. It was so small and innocuous; it was as if the war had passed it by. The man who ran the shop was old now but he remembered Sanders master's greedy granddaughter. He also told me that Vincent our driver was still alive but ill and in Jaffna hospital. I had planned to visit the hospital with the children anyway, as this was where I was born.

We located the once handsome Vincent but he was transformed into a skeletal form on a hospital bed. It turned out that a bomb had exploded some years before and Vincent had not only lost his car, which was his source of income, but his exquisite wife Lovely. They had one daughter and somehow he had got her out to Switzerland where she was doing well.

He was so poorly that his relatives communicated on his behalf and I left them the money Appah gave for him, as he would have no need of it. He passed away a few days later. Someone should have hung a sign on his hospital bed:

'Here lies another victim of our brutal civil war.'

A good man. A simple man. A man who never harmed anyone. People like us are not the victims. We rapidly reorganise ourselves and become established in other countries and climb or crawl to wherever we used to be.

We also travelled to Jaffna College; St John's where my great-great grandfather C.C. Handy's picture still hangs; the Kandaswami Temple; the fort and the now reconstructed Jaffna library. The people and their tenacity astounded me. One Catholic church had been bombed and the parishioners rebuilt a smaller version of it, with what remained intact. All buildings were bullet ridden.

I had to have an ice cream at Subbash café to cheer me up. If you said to people, 'This is terrible,' they smiled and said, 'Tomorrow will be better.' I had to stop myself from saying, 'Actually I think it might get worse.'

We visited my mother's cousin and had tea. Whatever they had they shared and whatever happened, they were not leaving. They were too old to adapt and they did not care for any country other than their own. We also went to the famous Mathagal Beach where we had all swum as children but I was told by a soldier that we could not unless we had a permit. He also indicated that mines may have been planted, so we risked losing our limbs.

We then travelled on to Atchuvely and my great-grandfather Joseph's little church was still fully functional. I could almost imagine him standing in the pulpit preaching in a passion and hear the echoes of Emily's voice in song. A plaque was erected in memory of them and Iyah's brother, Daniel, who died so young. I knew it to be my grandfather's work and remembered attending my brother's christening there, in better times.

Joseph and Emily were lying nearby and so we proceeded to the burial grounds. The driver was being vague and unhelpful again and left us some distance away, refusing to take his car any further.

We took our pictures but it was a most peculiar place strewn with bones and what looked like bits of cow. This was a very strange sight in Sri Lanka, where the cow is sacred. Our children instinctively disliked the place and were anxious to leave. I questioned the driver about it upon our return and he said quite casually that it was because of the landmines. He clearly thought he was driving some lunatics from abroad who threw caution to the wind.

On the last day we had to wake up at 3 a.m. and I told the man running the guest house not to bother with tea or breakfast. We would ruin his day and it was not necessary, as we had already paid the bill. At 3.15 a.m. there was a gentle tap on the door and he quietly placed all he had prepared in our rooms, smiled and left. This sort of dutiful and dignified behaviour was ever apparent around us. When I was awoken at anti-social hours in my job, the first thing I usually did was to swear.

My husband took pictures and videos of all we saw and did. Perhaps we could have promoted it as Gruesome Tours. The tour ended appropriately in the church yard of St James's. Great place to take the kids, I know. Certainly a day out that they would not forget. Here all my people lay in deep slumber. Grandaunts and uncles, my great-great-grandfather, my great-grandfather and amongst all the other Handys, my Iyah.

He had put himself there because he thought Harriet would join him but she had stood him up and had to be buried in Australia. I tried to explain to my children that we were not recent migrants to this land, as some would have them believe. We were not like 'Indians claiming a bit of Bradford' as the Sri Lankan government representative in the UK called us. My people, their people, had been here for thousands of years and Nallur was from whence the ancient Tamil kings had ruled their kingdom. There was a bullet-ridden archway nearby that we showed them, which was the entrance to their palace.

Graveyards are important places often undervalued and overlooked. In *Who do you think you are?* J.K. Rowling is taken to her grandfather's graveyard and to a lot of other places. Now I could have saved the broadcasting company a fortune and told them I know who she is! 'She's a millionaire author, clearly very bright and creative,' but it wasn't about that.

What we came from, is also who we are, not just what we achieve.

She was taken to a communal grave where her ancestor was buried and was clearly distressed and unable to make it better. All those years later, it still mattered.

I sent the children and my husband away for a little while and sat by my grandfather's grave. I said all I needed to him and dug up a piece of my land to take back with me. I had travelled a long way to find my grandfather but I should have known he was not there. I had been foolish, for he had been right by my side all along.

CHAPTER 17

# HOW TO
# DIE

There is a definite problem in the West about death. It is viewed as a disaster, a medical failure, something hideous to avoid. The truth is that death can be your release. It is not really something we can usually control and is part of life's cycle. Pneumonia used to be called 'the old man's friend' and often took the frailest away and spared them more suffering.

Now people need to be resuscitated, ventilated, and sign forms of consent to die. Instead of death being a simple event at the end of one's life, it has become an administrative nightmare. A guilt-fest for all concerned, apart from the dead person, who hopefully can't feel anything.

My brother was recently holidaying with his family in Cape Verde having a brief respite from his far too busy life. It was what he described as one of their 'veg out' holidays, sun, sea and sand, designed to recharge batteries. His bad luck however, the sea was not entirely safe and the flags were red or yellow but never green.

Patience is not one of his attributes and he became fed up waiting and so decided yellow was good enough. He had forgotten that he was not as young or as strong as he used to be. An enormous wave seemed to come from nowhere and raised him to the sky and then deposited him unceremoniously on to the sand with a bump. He fractured his coccyx and staved his finger, which served him right. He didn't have much time to feel sorry for himself, as before he knew it the sand was moving from under him and he was sucked out to sea.

In the distance his wife flicked through her magazine and the children continued building their sandcastles without a care. The Atlantic embraced him and dragged him down, down, deep to her bosom. He was for a second mesmerised by her, transfixed and unable to respond, he lay suspended and then it hit him. He was drowning. The tiger in him that had lain dormant roared and the memory of his family on the beach spurred his intent. His heart raced, his limbs beat, and he gasped out for air. He lived.

I hope this event will help to focus his mind on the important things in life. It is rare for an individual's last thoughts to involve the work they did not do, or the paper they did not write. It was not my brother's time, not yet.

After the Sri Lankan trip it became apparent that my father's health was failing. He put off going to the doctor until after Christmas and his wedding anniversary. I think he knew his diagnosis already and took it with dignity.

My mother sat in front of Appah and held his hands in hers and said, 'Where are you going my darling? Where are you going, leaving me?'

'What to do Ammah. When is a good time to die?'

I wanted to butt in, 'I know. One day after me, Dad. One day, but not today.'

You can learn a lot from someone's life and you can learn a lot from their death as well. I wrote an article about it all in a journal and it was published. I think it was the finest thing I have ever written and so rather than changing it in any way and because any short cut is always good for me, I have copied it.

*My father was a big man, in more ways than one! He was my mentor, guide and friend, on a personal and professional level. The last lesson he taught me, was how to die. There has been much in the BMJ and press lately on death, care of the elderly, concerns about patient choice and dignity. My father chose a low tech, minimal intervention, home death. He and death had a long relationship. He knew death intimately, as a retired geriatrician and because he had cheated death already.*

*He had a cerebral haemorrhage thirteen years before, when he was working flat out as a consultant. He had a massive insult to his brain and his case notes recorded 'no CPR', with our agreement. On that occasion he won the battle and walked out of hospital eight weeks later to spar another day. Life was not easy after this event but he and my mother managed independently, travelled abroad extensively and saw five grandchildren, who were a delight to him.*

*In December last year death visited him again. He developed a chest infection that seemed to respond to antibiotics but then returned with right sided pleuritic pain. He conceded to further investigation. Our local chest physician was wonderful and knowing his mobility issues organised everything on one day and told us he had a 5 cm lesion in his right apex, extensive mediastinal, adrenal and possibly liver involvement. She treated him as a colleague/patient and discussed the options available, which were very limited, only palliative and, at best, would extend his life by a few weeks.*

*My father, in discussion with the doctor, decided not to have a biopsy and another painful trip to hospital. He felt it would be academic, as he saw no benefit in going for palliative treatment. He told us all to return to work as normal, as he intended to continue with his daily routine. He informed only his siblings, and he wanted as little fuss as possible. He was a man of faith and believed quite simply that his time had come. Now death would have him but unlike everyone around, he shed no tears. He gave my mother a quiet time to adjust to the news.*

*A few weeks later my father lost his vision and casually informed us that he probably now had cerebral spread. We were not to call his GP out unnecessarily, as there would be little she could do, but he requested a prescription for dexamethasone as a last attempt to regain his vision. At this point I became distressed at work and my kind colleagues advised me to stop.*

*We had two precious weeks and talked non-stop about how it would be, this dying. How he would like it to be. He spoke to my mother on how to manage without him, and organised his finances. He got me to purchase his burial plot. During this time he managed to partake in his grandsons' birthdays and Mother's Day celebrations. He enjoyed what life he had left with his family and did not wait upon death. A fortnight later he went off his feet. My mother, sister and I could not lift him, so we called our brother, who then became the human hoist. He would put Dad in a wheelchair and we carried on as before. We were all five together now, as we used to be. It was a bittersweet time. Our father kept to his daily routine in spite of increasing pain, breathlessness and lethargy.*

*The GP visited weekly and gave Dad morphine. He tried it once but became constipated and less able to assist my brother with transfer. He decided to do without and instead managed with a combination of paracetamol and ibuprofen. I must admit that had it been me, I would have consumed the morphine by the bellyful but I suspected that he had a plan. He wanted at all times to be in charge of himself and with three children, all doctors, had a fear of what great ideas we would cook up between us!*

*Next his renal output diminished and he developed gout. He was not keen on further medication for fear of side effects and suggested elevation and ice, a good old-fashioned remedy. He developed hip and shoulder pain, so we massaged him. My siblings and I procured various continence aids, which lay concealed in the boot of my car, as he would surely sooner or later need these, but he didn't. His appetite was poor and he declined build-up drinks, so I learnt to make bread and butter pudding, caramel pudding and all the egg and milk-rich treats my grandmother made and that he loved as a boy. I had to seriously brush up on my wartime cookery skills.*

*One day he told me he needed his bed. It was only 7 p.m. and he was veering off his schedule. He insisted, however, that I get my brother and then we knew that the end was in sight. After saying goodnight to us all, he finally said he would take his morphine. It was to have a profound impact on one so debilitated, without previous exposure, and within 36 hours he was gone.*

*The Scotsman had 20 obituaries that week. Only two of these deaths were at home and both were doctors. I think my father knew how to die. He faced death, as he faced all issues in life, full on. No doubt his own medical knowledge helped him and we were lucky, in that all the doctors who attended him were so mindful of his wishes. He had his low tech, minimal intervention, no counselling, few drugs death. In some ways he was a simple man and he had a simple death. Sadly so few of our patients do. Perhaps we need to encourage them more. Fight for life by all means but when the end comes, precious time should not be wasted on would-be cures, holy grails, net searches and trips to hospital!*

*Death is a certainty in every patient's life and we should be helping them face this final event with dignity.*
*My father taught me well. He cheated death again for he had no fear.*

(Articles from *The British Journal of General Practice* are provided here courtesy of Royal College of General Practitioners)

If you think you are going to die soon and you want to be buried, I would rush out and buy a plot if I were you. Good land is scarce and most people are cremated now. As my father was insistent on being buried, I had quite a time of it, but I found him a good hole in the end.

We siblings purchased an enormous granite stone and had a palm tree carved on it. We said he came from Ceylon and we use the same quote as on Iyah's grave 'In faith is the victory.'

Appah would have thought this a bit big and flashy but he wasn't there to object. Before he died, we checked with him if it was okay for us all to get in with him, when the time came. He thought this hilarious and had no objection. It's a great leveller seeing your own burial place. I tell myself not to take problems too seriously, as in the end we are all worm feast and my hole is waiting for me.

My nephew, Sam, has a very long Tamil surname and middle name; he is concerned that he won't fit in. He says we will have to get a separate short, fat stone just for him.

You could argue that all of this is the height of arrogance. If everyone wanted to be buried, the world would be covered in gravestones.

My father was different because he was one of the first who came to this land. That's what we were trying to say, the man from Ceylon. Just as his father and siblings worked over one hundred years for Jaffna College, he and his children have served the NHS for over a hundred years.

The graveyard is near a church and a school and he has a sunny spot. My mother smothers his grave in flowers and draws attention to him. He would have cringed with embarrassment and said something sarcastic if he could.

After the first year the earth about him sank badly and they had to fix it all again. I thought it an omen. No heaven for you Samuel. How could it be heaven without her?

They do a tour of the site for the Edinburgh Festival called the 'Great and the Good of Edinburgh' as many famous people are also buried there. My sister and mother waited patiently one August as a bus load of Japanese tourists stood around Appah's grave and had a discussion.

My mother visited my father's grave every day for two years. After this, she too had a stroke and then needed us to take her, so once a week was more than enough for us.

The lads that work there all know her well and tell her all their troubles. She is like a grandmother figure to them. They are a formidable looking bunch but she has them eating out of her hand.

My grandparents were both nearly ninety when they died, although they had full cream milk and no statins. The next generation of Sri Lankans took two or three decades off that. My brother used to see them in ITU. Apparently the diagnosis is often a heart attack or stroke. I would give them a Victorian diagnosis – 'melancholia.'

Every Sunday we go to church, see Appah and then all have Sunday lunch together as a family. We just do what we used to do in Ceylon and these weekly meals bind us together as a family in good and bad times. My mother cannot cook much anymore and the burnt offerings are barely palatable but that's irrelevant.

Being all mostly doctors, the first hour is spent relatively cordially, supporting each other and bemoaning NHS changes. Invariably dissent breaks out on some topic or other and it's definitely time to go home, only to do it all again the following week.

# CHAPTER 18

# THE GERMANS ARE COMING

We siblings refer to my mother's family as the Saras. Saravanamuthu is a hideous mouthful and, furthermore, this is inaccurate, as Hindus do not retain their surnames as Christians do.

The Saras are an impulsive, generous, wild, undisciplined lot. Even Nesi's children are the same, so as my mother and aunt had different fathers, my maternal grandmother's genetics must account for these interesting traits!

When all the troubles broke out, Nesi and Wicky continued to live in Mathagal as before. They had four children, two boys and two girls. The eldest boy was called Siri and he was my hero. He was in the army for a while and very dashing in uniform and about a decade older than us.

My cousin Siri and his siblings were lucky enough to have a Sinhala second name and had a Buddhist father, so could easily have chosen an easy life as such. Not so my cousins. They were appalled by all of the anti-Tamil goings on and I am sure were up to every trick in the book and took a pro-Tamil stance.

I once tried to talk to my cousin about this but he would not tell me what he had done and instead winked at me and smiled. I have heard all sorts of rumours about them and their activities in Sri Lanka.

Nesi had not lost her tongue, however, and did not spare her children her wrath or hand. She literally beat them into submission and shipped three of them to Germany. The eldest of her four children was already married and not part of the three musketeers.

Having messed up their studies due to civil unrest and their own solutions to it, they had trouble getting decent jobs in Germany. They stuck together and did any job they could. Jointly they eventually gathered enough money and moved into a three in a block, where each sibling took up one floor.

I am sure, like every family, they have had their good and bad times but through it all they have united and supported each other. When one cousin's husband nearly died from an accident at work, the others worked twice as hard to support them and shared meals, hospital shifts, child care et cetera. If I had this arrangement with my sibling, fratricide would have ensued.

Siri took all this responsibility on board, as well as helping out any Sri Lankans, Tamil or Sinhala that came within his radar and needed assistance. Though never well off financially, their whole approach to life had always been 'Our cup is half full; plenty for sharing.'

Wicky seemed initially immune from all that was going on around him as his reputation as a good man of longstanding in the area preceded him. One day he was not so lucky. Some Tiger boys got hold of him. Shocked to see a Sinhala man wandering about 'their territory' they detained and questioned him. Unhappy with his responses to their questions, they started to rough him up a bit, before someone stopped them and linked him to my infamous cousins.

This event unsettled Wicky terribly, as he had done nothing to deserve this treatment. Throughout his decades in Mathagal in the north, he had been neighbourly and helpful.

He demanded to go to his home, to Galle, in the south and Nesi was unable to reassure him and so agreed to the trip. After so many years living on Tamil territory, in the end he wanted his land, and his people. Once there, he still seemed very distracted and on crossing the road was knocked down and died.

Nesi went to Germany for a while and my mother was able to visit her briefly with my sister. Nesi had a lifetime of being the boss and could not re-adjust to a foreign land. When she, too, grew old and frail, she returned to Sri Lanka for the last chapter in her tale.

Siri's children speak German, as does my daughter, so communication through them is the way forward, as my Tamil is as poor as his English.

My cousin came to visit my mother recently and he looked as sprightly as ever. He is a man who enjoys life and lives for the day with gusto. The Saras are noisy, tactile and full of life. He proceeded to tell us that the German doctors were a little concerned about his renal function and diabetes. When I glanced at his biochemistry results, it became apparent that his renal function was minimal. I was astonished as people in his state of health are generally sitting motionless, depressed and exhausted.

'You're quite ill and need an urgent transplant,' I said dumbfounded.

'Illness is in your head,' was the response.

When he came in such a hurry to see my mother, it was not her longevity he was thinking of but his.

My cousin awaits a transplant. Because he has been such a generous and selfless person all his life, he has had quite a few offers. He still has not found a match however. Many of his Sinhala cousins have come forward already and his Tamil cousins are thinking about it!

His main concern is that he does not want to be off work too long as his children are at university and require his financial support. He does not want them to graduate in debt or have to work whilst they study.

My cousin is unusual as he is one of my heroes and still alive. Most of my other heroes are dead old men, which must say something about me.

The greatest exception to this, being alive and female is Aung San Suu Kyi. She is best described as Burma's living symbol of hope and democracy. I like seeing Burma on television, as it looks so much like Sri Lanka full of natural beauty, lush and green.

Aung San Suu Kyi has the face of an angel, beneath which clearly lies a will of steel. They said of the late Queen mother that she was 'velvet glove and iron fist' and I think this lady is much the same. During David Cameron's visit to Burma, he was clearly in awe of this genteel Burmese icon.

I would offer her Sri Lankan citizenship, if I could. I have a feeling she would say no, but we really need someone like her. This lady has no fear.

My other fearless hero was Lasantha Wickrematunge, a Sinhala gentleman who was the former editor of *The Sunday Leader* in Sri Lanka. He reported the truth and could only be silenced in death. He wrote a letter, published upon his demise, naming his killer.

These people have an amazing calling. What made them sacrifice their families and their whole life's work for their country? I am happy to be average.

I want to grow to a ripe old age and I know that cowards live longer than heroes. I don't have it in me to leave my children in pursuit of a cause. I tell myself that my children are my calling.

My last hero is Jon Snow. He has fire in his eyes and has been relentless in his pursuit of the truth about the Sri Lankan situation. My other heroes have a vested interest in their causes, they were called by their country, but Lanka has no connection for him, as far as I am aware. He is just a man in search of the truth. I wrote to him once thanking him for all he had done for us. He did not write back but I suspect he gets a lot of fan mail and possibly hate mail as well. Perhaps he burns all the letters good and bad, so that he does not get distressed or have them sway his judgement.

I have always wanted to be a heroine myself but am far too comfortable to do anything selfless or rash. I am filled with anger at all that has passed but I have done nothing to help. My cousin Siri has continued to visit Sri Lanka and do what he can to support as many as he can.

My sister has never tired of telling me what to do. She says anger and resentment are negative emotions that will eat me up and help no one.

'Make your pen your sword,' she instructs me.

Most of what I have written about the political situation in Sri Lanka has never been published, or has been so altered as to be unrecognisable. So it was that I started writing this. The brain fogs with the passage of years and things good and bad lie forgotten. I cannot bring back the dead and I agree that we must move forward with the Sri Lankan problem but first we must acknowledge what happened and all take responsibility for it.

Siri's children say they are German. My children say they are Scottish and I say nothing because, though once I was so proud, now I am ashamed of my country.

The Sri Lankan population is tiny but we have the seventeenth largest army in the world. This does not bode well for anyone left on the island. Journalists and anyone opposing the government disappear without opposition. People are so pleased that the civil war is over, that they do not seem to notice that they are rapidly becoming a police state.

When you arrive at the airport you are warned not to criticise the government. So much for democracy. Can you imagine a big sign at Heathrow saying 'Do not say anything derogatory about our devoted Dave?' People are frightened on all sides and do not question what is going on. I am reminded of the famous saying by Pastor Martin Niemollar:

'First they came for the communists and I did not speak out because I was not a communist. Then they came for the trade unionists and I did not speak out because I was not a unionist. Then they came for the Jews and I did not speak out because I was not a Jew. Then they came for me and there was no one left to speak out for me.'

The Germans are an interesting people. All those that have ever worked with me have had a super work ethic and been so straightforward it was refreshing.

When I was in school in the seventies, some of them came over on an exchange and we were asked to write down the top ten things we associated with Germany.

My first response was 'Nazi'. I felt really bad writing that but it was true. Thirty years later I think I would say, 'Vorsprung durch Technik,' as in the Audi advert. It is possible for a people to make a big mistake but they have acknowledged it, and we have all moved on.

The Germans have been very kind to a lot of my countrymen and provided jobs, homes, hospitality and safety. Many other countries have done likewise – Norway, Canada and Australia. There continues to be a steady drip of people out of Sri Lanka and an active settling of Sinhala people on Tamil land. In one generation our numbers have been halved and I think in another, we will be no more.

There is a story in the Bible that I love. King Solomon the wise is presented with two weeping women and one baby. The first woman points to the second and says, 'She has stolen my baby.'

The second weeps louder against claims that her child died accidently in sleep, and that she took the live child and laid in its place the dead one.

Solomon the Great says, 'Bring me a sword.'

'Cut the child in two, and give half to one mother, and half to the other.'

The second woman says, 'Divide it as the King has ordained.'

'Pray give her the child. I beg you do not kill it,' screams the other.

Thus the real mother was revealed to King Solomon.

I say my sister is right; anger and resentment are negative emotions. It was our birth right, our Ur, but take it, take it all and let there be peace.

# CHAPTER 19

# OUR CHILDREN

*Sleep peacefully now my child*
*I hope that you go away*
*To a place where your dreams can play*
*Wipe all the tears from your eyes*
*There is a sky of blue*
*This is your time of truth*

*Like a bird high on the wind*
*May you fly away*
*Like a snowfall in the spring*
*may your cares melt away*
*CHILD, innocent child*
*our hope lies inside*
*your starry eyes*
*my innocent child*

*Hero, now that you are free*
*You have no need to fear*

*so go out and find your smile*
*Like a candle in the stream*
*May you float away*
*Like a feather on the breeze*
*May you blow away*

Mark Owen

I have six children. Technically some of them belong to my siblings, but I say they are all mine. Photographs of them are mounted on my wall at work and patients are astonished at how I have managed to keep working, with this brood to care for.

They are the most wonderful thing that has happened to us and I don't know where they came from. Each is very different from the other and they are quite united, especially against the oldies.

Our first boy Dan is the most sensitive and caring. He has his grandfather's eyes and way of looking at the world, the same dry sense of humour . Rohi is our bright shining star, ever optimistic and forgiving. She generally edits all I write and say. Sam is our entrepreneur and entertainer. He has turned his home into a zoo, which I am charged with looking after whenever he goes on holiday, which is a lot. Rajan is organised and reliable; he has the tidiest room in the house and does not like anyone tampering with his things. He reminds me of an old gentleman I used to know. Simmy is an honest and upstanding little citizen and fortunately has taken after her mother. She is our first Sanders girl. Finally just when we had all but given up, we got our Sanders boy too. He is just like my brother David, only much, much worse.

I was sorry that my father did not meet him. He would have roared with laughter and told my brother something like, 'Vengeance is mine, sayeth the Lord!'

My brother saw nothing wrong with calling his son Daniel as well.

'That's ridiculous,' complained Rosh 'what a limited family, to keep choosing the same name.'

'They have different surnames and live in different cities,' was the reply. Some people have no common sense.

The net result of this is that Daniel two is called Squirt.

'Squirt, do you love me?' I ask.

'Yes,' he says hurriedly and unconvincingly, as he tries to run off.

'Squirt, will you look after me when I get old?'

'YES!'

'Squirt, will you carry me, if I cannot walk?'

'NO! You're too heavy. Ammah will be dead by then, so you can use her stick.' Since Squirt is only four years old, this is a pretty smart answer. I think I will hold out for Simmy instead if I ever need someone to care for me.

The children draw us together. Even if we can sometimes do without meeting, they insist on it and each looks after the other. The calendar is punctuated by our gathering for birthdays, Christmas and annual trips to our timeshare home near Oban, all of which is practically compulsory.

It will be fascinating to see what paths their lives take. They have little understanding or real interest in the Sri Lankan problems. There is an irritation about being forced to watch programmes on television whilst the oldies shake their heads and weep. They tire of our reminiscing and stories.

You cannot deny your heritage, however. Sooner or later it comes back to haunt you.

When my father was dying he wanted his people. His own siblings were too frail themselves to see him but his cousins and our cousins came. It was a comfort to him. Relatives can of course be a great irritant but they have usually travelled the longest journey with you, and as you get older and friends are fewer, they can be a vital link with past and present.

One of my father's cousins had not been seen for decades but popped up unexpectedly and cheered us all, when things were bleak. He is one of those eternally young at heart people like Harriet. He arrived at the time of Rajan's eighth birthday. My father told him,

'Rajan would like you to stay for his birthday, have one last drink with me.' Rajan was eight then and really could not have cared less but it was Dad's way of saying stay a while. It really was the last drink too!

Dad's other cousin and wife live in London and they have always kept in touch regularly and especially when we needed it. We attended this cousin's seventieth birthday party last year, which was on a glorious autumnal English day. Everyone was standing about eating and drinking in the grounds of the country club, whilst the river flowed gently behind us and the trees were golden in the autumnal light.

He was standing a little separately surveying the scene, feasting his eyes on a lifetime of family and friends gathered together. It is at such moments that life stops for an instant and you take stock.

A fiery little redhead shot past him. Any observer would never link this dignified tall, slim Ceylonese gentleman with the very Celtic looking child but she was his granddaughter.

One day, if it rains a lot, and there is nothing to do, maybe she will read a book about her grandfather's people. She may even get round to reading this, if she truly is very, very bored.

I have been brought up to know not only my cousins but my second and third cousins as well. The children think this is comical and quite unnecessary. They are much more interested in their friends whom they can pick and choose. They feel distant relations are something inflicted on them that they would like to avoid. On the plus side, we have a relative in virtually every country in the world, an unexpected bonus of civil war and an asset to our 'gap year' loving brigade.

Sri Lanka is a small country with a small population but the largest percentage of expats of any country in the world.

I worry about the children and how they will negotiate the east and west within them. If they cling on to the spirit more than the body and hold on to family values, that's probably good enough for me. They are sure to play 'pick and mix' and if they are clever, they can have the best of all.

My daughter tells me that when she gets married she will never wear a sari. Bed sheets do nothing for the figure! I become exasperated and tell her it's not about the outfit, it's about making the statement of who you are. When she can no longer squeeze into her wedding dress, I will always be able to get into my sari.

My son tells me he has decided to marry a non-Christian, that way he gets every Christmas with his cousins and his own family. That's my boy.

We took for granted when we grew up in Ceylon the network of parents, grandparents, cousins, aunts and uncles around us. They formed a cushion against the trials and tribulations in life. If you were sick, some relative would appear to help. If you were broke, a few rupees were discreetly pushed into your sweaty palm. If you were sad, someone was sure to turn up and tell you to pull yourself together. There are no mental health problems in Lanka, as this would reflect badly on the family.

There were codes of behaviour instilled over generations. Of course this could all be quite oppressive at times but systems work. Too much choice is a bad thing and can lead to confusion. If I go into a shop with too many things, I end up with a headache having purchased nothing. Maybe it's just me.

My grandfather taught me to stick to a routine. He believed in taking care of body and soul and in troubled times his systems and routine sustained him. By some random act of birth I have been fortunate to have had so many good teachers in my life. Some people are very bright and work out volumes by themselves. I do 'follow' really well. Others are unlucky and have never had the love and nurturing I have had. It can then be confusing to navigate your own path without a map.

My brother used to call me 'Dad's little disciple' with some disdain. I thought it a compliment. If a chap was intelligent and had a ninety-five per cent chance of being right, why on earth would I bother thinking for myself? I had a good sleep for forty years.

Then you get the challenging ones, I mention no names, those who see and know the paths to take but just go another way for the hell of it. These are your geniuses or fools.

I try to explain all of this to the children, who find my little ways rigid and comical. I stuff a cooked breakfast into their mouths as they rush out the door to school complaining that nobody else does this anymore. Their friends are so lucky – they get breakfast bars or better still nothing at all!

CHAPTER 20

# THE KILLING FIELDS
# OF SRI LANKA

On the fourteenth of June 2011 Channel Four dropped a bomb on Sri Lankans throughout the world by airing its programme *The Killing Fields of Sri Lanka*. This programme detailed what happened in the last days of the war between the Sri Lankan army and the Tamil Tigers. The civilian casualties exposed were staggering.

We were horrified and, in the words of the son of former President Chandrika, 'Ashamed to call ourselves Sri Lankan.' We have all played our part in this carnage –those who took part and those who pretended it was not happening.

I drove to my mother's house utterly distraught. I saw my cousin's face in every victim. My poor mother, though frail and muddled sat me on her lap and said, 'What to do *pillai*?'

A few days later I fired off letters to the Prime Minister, my church, and the BMA, as many doctors had been tortured and bombed as in Syria.

I have written several letters to different governments in Britain over the years and their responses are all the same. Some minion is given the task of writing back and I am sure that the PM never sees a word of it. The usual platitudes, 'We take your concerns seriously,' but, 'have to consider British interests abroad.' They probably have a standardised letter that they send to nuts like me and change a few words around to personalise it, a bit like my kids 'thank you for my amazing present' birthday letters. The BMA had already printed a few articles on the matter and were clear that they would do no more.

My minister at church received a response from the church's representatives in Sri Lanka, however, which made the most sense. They were fully aware of what had gone on but in the spirit of moving forward and, because people were terrified, they were not keen to reopen this wound at present. They lived in the hope that one day justice would be done. I understood the wisdom of their stance and was not going to become another 'armchair politician.'

None of my articles were published and no one answered my question, 'Why is it we go to war with Iraq but play cricket with Sri Lanka?' No prizes for the obvious answer.

We are a small country far from America and without oil. It could be argued that we brought this disaster upon ourselves. The world, having initially been sympathetic to the Tiger cause, has, over the years, turned against all terrorist organisations. Fair enough, but it is rare for a government to turn against its own people and that is where we are unique. Terrorists account to no one and notoriously compromise their principles and standards. Governments, supposedly elected by their people, should aspire to be better.

I promised myself that even if no one else would publish it, I would still sing my unsung song:

> *Yesterday I watched* The Killing Fields of Sri Lanka *by Jon Snow on Channel Four. It was on way past my bedtime, at 11 p.m., and I was trying not to watch it but in the end could not help myself.*
>
> *Deep down inside, I knew what I would see and every horror you could imagine unfolded in front of my eyes. Much of the story was told by a British/Tamil student of biomedical science. She happened to have been on holiday at the time, poor soul. She would certainly have the experience of a lifetime!*
>
> *The BMJ during this time published a number of items, sent in by medical colleagues from Sri Lanka, detailing their concerns that UN regulations were being contravened and that hospitals and doctors were being bombed and targeted. They bravely kept to their posts and*

continued their work as best as they could. When I go to work each day, I expect a great many things but certainly not to be shot at.

The programme informed me that 40,000 people may have been disposed of. It was much like the Nazi/Jewish thing but with less international interest. But this happened only two years ago. I was born and brought up there. I know the government is economical with the truth and had been following events closely, though I chose not to respond. People like me from well off, middle class, Sri Lankan families always find a way out. There will always be a plane or a train for us. I have contacts and there is no way I would be found beaten, raped, murdered and dumped in a truck.

I could have gone to Sri Lanka to help and many medical colleagues did. They clearly 'had a calling'. I, however, have relatively young children, a sick elderly mother, and a number of other reasons why I could not do this.

In one scene at the 'hospital' a man is sitting on the floor gently caressing his fourteen year old son's head. He runs his fingers through his hair and over the small of his back, just as I do to my boy, when he is sleepy and lets me. They have been air-raided by government troops and his son is bleeding to death. The good doctor can only offer words of comfort; he has no facilities, no medicines and no blood to give.

The biomedical student is asked to hold a six-year-old down. She has become an emergency 'doctor'. He has had his arm and leg blown off and, unless these are amputated, he has no hope. She does a good job before she faints and they think he survived.

When I sit in my surgery contemplating QOF points and the minor irritations of general practice, it is easy to underestimate our value and skills.

I am a Christian (most unfashionable I know), as such I will try not to hate. It is not constructive but I have contempt for those who have carried out these acts of barbarism and cruelty. However, I reserve my greatest contempt for people like me: the silent ones, the good ones, who pretend not to know what is happening and go about their daily 'duties'.

This article is dedicated to the selfless doctors who stayed and did not run away. They had no hospital, no staff and no equipment but simply did the best they could. Also to the pretty biochemical student. I have an

*MBChB and you do not but you have proved yourself to be a better
doctor than I will ever be.*

There is a big effort currently to pretend that all is well in Sri Lanka. Tamils
and Sinhalese alike are returning to see what it is like. What happened to
their lands and homes? They stay in some of the plush new hotels springing
up at a terrific pace. There is a determination to bring back tourism and say,
'All is well now the Tigers have gone,' or 'Come to the Garden of Eden,
Serendib, The Resplendent Isle.'

Watch the people, however, and see how they are frightened to speak out
or contradict the government. As we have seen in history again and again,
'absolute power' sooner or later leads to 'absolute corruption'. If you dare to
venture out of tourist heaven, count the number of army personnel or policemen you encounter. Why, it puts the lack of British bobbies on the beat to
shame.

The citizens unfortunate enough to still live there have to pretend and
because journalists are not free to report the truth, they may be in some happy
ignorance or denial. That is not our position, we are on the outside looking
in and so in some ways more equipped to see clearly what is going on.
My own feeling is that Sri Lanka is like a diseased old prostitute given a great
makeover and up for sale to the highest bidder.

I used to love the rich ochre soil of Ceylon, my country. When I went to
see my grandfather's grave I stole a fist full of it and put it in a silver box,
which I keep near my bed. When I open the box and peer at it now, instead
of thinking of the land of my fathers, my *Ur*, I see its red colour and think of
blood.

We used to mockingly call Sri Lanka 'Ireland in the sun' but now Ireland is
better. Maybe one day we will be better too. The Church's representative wrote
to me saying, 'Pray for us' and that is all I can do, and what I do, every night.

## CHAPTER 21

# YE'LL TAK THE HIGH ROAD

*Ye'll tak the high road*
*And I'll tak the low road*
*And I'll be in Scotland before ye*

'What ARE you doing?'

'Writing a book.'

'Yes. You used to do that when you were a little girl.'

'Hopefully there's a bit more to this one.'

'Now let me see. Good God! Have you asked all these people if they mind?'

'No way. They would either say no or alter it. It would be turned into a politically correct sham.'

'What a stroke of genius. You can alienate all your relatives in one shot. I think some of these details need corroboration, some of this is hearsay not fact.'

'I don't care, it's my version of events.'

'How very convenient for you.'

'It's like a van Gogh. His scenes were an interpretation of what he saw and felt. It would be like saying to him those flowers are a bit scruffy, they are painted inaccurately and in a childlike fashion.'

'This is certainly written in a childlike fashion. You are clearly emulating that particular trait of the old master. I hope you've checked your spelling, it was always atrocious. It all seems a bit disorganised.'

'That's how I think.'

'I'm fully aware of that unfortunate fact.'

'You should be doing this, not me.'

'No thank you. Unlike you, self-promotion was never my strong point. I hope I am not in this inspired work of genius.'

'No. Nothing to do with you.'

'Well that's a great relief. How is your mother these days?'

'What can I say? Girlfriend is driving us all round the bend.'

'Don't be rude.'

'Thanks for dumping her off on us.'

'Dying is not generally a voluntary act is it?'

'She goes on and on and on about you. She is driving us nuts.'

'Yes, we were special ...'

'It's certainly especially annoying. Feel free to remove her at any point. Then again, you're probably having the time of your life.'

'You were always very critical about your mother.'

'I don't do sweet little old ladies. They usually turn out to be fake.'

'You always underestimated her.'

'Not at all. I think she is one of the most terrifying people I have ever met."

'I think she is doing rather well.'

'You would.'

'She is an Asian lady who has had several strokes with little vision or balance and in cognitive decline, living alone.'

'What does that mean? We do a lot you know.'

'I know that.'

'This is not Ceylon. There are no servants, though I sometimes feel like one.'

'You have always been a dutiful daughter.'

'Definitely my starring role. I can feel a BUT coming on.'

'Do less and enjoy more.'

'Zorba the Greek.'

'Yes, be like Zorba. Enjoy it all. Stop taking life so seriously. Your mother and I enjoyed every day, good and bad. If you see no good in the day, the fault is yours.'

'Thanks for that. Really helpful as always.'

'You are welcome.'

'I have to get on now. I want to get this finished and move on.'

'Always in a hurry.'

'Some of us don't have all the time in the world.'

'Well, I better get going. Be seeing you real soon.'

'Funny. I don't think so. I have work to do.'

'That's my girl, so you do.'

'Dad.'

'Mmmm.'

'I miss you, you were my island. Come back.'

'Stop that. What did I tell you?'

'Sanders girls don't cry.'

'Ever.'

The thing is, I really hate tea. I'd rather have Scottish 'water' any day. *Bhilas* are hideous and cricket is a bore. I hate watching any sport but if I had to watch something, rugby is tolerable.

I have swapped islands. It's taken a while and my love marriage to Sri Lanka never worked out that well but the arranged marriage is on firmer foundations. I expected nothing and got much more. Finally I have found what I have always been searching for, contentment. It just turned out to be on a different island.

I adore the seasons, the promise of spring, the beauty of summer, the bounty of autumn and the cooler colours of winter. I can no longer imagine a life with only two seasons.

The colours of the tropics, like the saris and sarongs are dramatic and exotic but the colours here are more subtle but equally lovely, less harsh on the eye.

Few things can be more beautiful than the Scottish mountains, lochs and countryside. You are never far from water or the sea. I love the dour foreboding hills; they remind me that man is but a small creature passing through. The land is forever.

Everything is free in Scotland. There is a Calvinistic ethos still. All men are and can hope to be equal. Education and health are free. We can criticise what we have and aspire to make it better but try living without it. I think the NHS is the finest organisation in the world and am proud to be a part of it.

I do wish politicians would stop meddling with it all the time and turning it into a political football. Care of the elderly is free and to paraphrase Gandhi 'the greatness of a nation can be measured by its treatment of its frailest'.

We complain in Britain about our governments and the press. It is true that in all walks of life there will always be the corrupt and self-seeking but many people still work for the common good. If you really want to see corruption, go to Sri Lanka, they can show you a thing or two.

I read an article that stated that only fifteen per cent of the world has a free press. How lucky we are that we have a voice. British broadcasting and its uncompromising coverage of world issues, is another fine example of what is great about Britain.

I embrace it all – Burns, J.K. Rowling, the Proclaimers, Rab C, tartan, ceilidhs, the Loch Ness monster and the haggis roaming wild on the hills.

I love the fact that there are not too many people in Scotland. I can escape to open spaces quickly and even our motorways are quaint and not that busy. We are so well placed geographically that we can fly with ease to any part of the world and yet, being an island, we are a little apart. It is a land of peace, prosperity and in the words of William Wallace, or maybe Mel Gibson 'freedom'.

We can grumble about racism here but many immigrants have had greater opportunities in this foreign soil than in their own homeland. When the British had their colonies, they sometimes lived apart and did not assimilate with their host nations. Today many communities live in Britain as if they were in their country of origin. This is a truly limited existence. If you think you have nothing to learn from the indigenous people, you are arrogant and need to go back to your roots. You are clearly on a shallow learning curve.

I have equal disdain for those who pretend to be what they are not. 'Pick and mix' is definitely the way forward. No one nation is better than another. Like our children they are all different and have something special to offer and varied irritating traits.

I get a little anxious about Scottish independence. We are a small country and if we did not have our cousins across the border, would rapidly become insular. I have seen some of this behaviour before, this is how it starts. I do not want to see it again.

We have our part English, part Scottish, part German queen to bind us. She has an amazing work ethic and whether you are a royalist or not, she cannot be denied as one of the greatest queens that ever reigned. When we first came from Ceylon, I used to stand for the national anthem but never sing it. Now I sing too but if I'm honest never quite manage 'send her victorious'. I ask myself what I would do if Britain went to war with Sri Lanka; it would be hard but I would support the United Kingdom.

Even the greatest cynic must have been moved when seeing the Royal Wedding, The Queen's Diamond Jubilee and Olympic ceremony. Were we not all proud to be British then?

Our house is beautiful. It has double gates for cars and a single gate for people on foot. There are cherry trees that blossom in the front and apple trees at the back. We have planted a palm tree also and though it struggles with the cold and wind, it is firmly rooted now. My husband gifted me two pink climbing roses by the entrance of our house and no one is allowed to cut the flowers.

When I sit in my dining room, I see people's heads over the wall, instead of the legs I used to see under the partition in Guru Vasa. Sometimes the heads are familiar and turn to wave at me. I wave back and smile.

We have a veranda in the back and it is covered over with glass, to adapt to the Scottish climate. The garden has taken a lot of work but we have selected hardy heathers, hebes, rhododendrons and grasses that can withstand the wild east coast winds. We have a small vegetable plot and I love to grow and eat what we produce. One of these days, if I can overcome my excreta phobia, we may even get some chickens.

I am lucky to have such a comfortable life. I work hard and serve my patients, friends and neighbours. These are my people now. I am the family's personal organiser. I love to cook and entertain and have them all about me. I experiment with some of my mother's old Ceylonese recipes, some Indian vegetarian ones and steal ideas from *Come Dine with Me.*

We are lucky to have many good friends and neighbours who come and go. It is a busy house. Sometimes the children's cousins will gate-crash our dinner parties and deafen our guests with the fighting and noise.

I have a dear friend who lives across the street. We go to a weekly Pilates class with a bunch of riotous middle-aged ladies. It is our girl time. We set the world to rights and have long discussions on whatever is topical, whilst doing the minimal amount of exercise possible. The teacher has given up trying to 'sculpt our bodies.' I love to walk and am lucky enough to be able to put on my walking boots and in ten minutes be by the water.

The children have presented me with an iPod so that I can listen to my favourite tunes without annoying them. I walk past waterfalls and rivers and boats on the Firth of Forth. The water is dirty and cold, only tourists who don't know what they are doing get into it. The warning signs are clear; perhaps they cannot read or are not bothered.

I used to tell my children about the beaches in Sri Lanka and how spectacular the sea was to swim and fish in. Priorities change, this water is not so good but I can swim if I want to and I don't need a permit. I can walk where I want to and I don't feel unsafe.

The little brother turned out to be less dim than I thought. He was appointed as the youngest professor of gastroenterology in Britain. Some of the Aussie cousins are professors too. He works way too hard but he loves it and gives of his best.

One of his patients was an elderly gentleman, a regular at his clinic who had the unnerving habit of staring at him, almost rudely at times. Getting the patient better was a major feat. At his last appointment the patient grabbed my brother's hand, fixed his eyes with a piercing gaze and said, 'This Sinhala man thanks this Tamil boy for all he has done.'

The sister and husband are in discussion with the Scottish government. They are not in any trouble. One is trying to improve eye referrals by sending optician's digital photographs straight to specialists. This means you do not have to go through your GP and I am more than happy about that, less work for me is always good. She can save the government a lot of money.

The husband says half the people with ADHD (Attention Deficit Hyperactivity Disorder) do not grow out of it and that there is no service for these poor souls. The condition is present in twenty per cent of our prison population. Many of them end up addicted to alcohol or drugs and join the ranks of the unemployed. He has already turned so many people's lives around. It is inspiring work helping those that need it most, instead of those who shout the loudest.

My sister has bought a house nearby from whence she can supervise me. It stands on a hill with a good bit of land overlooking trees and reminds us of the bungalows in the Ceylon tea estates. Oddly the previous owners, who were from the Hodge family, had a connection with Ceylon where their father worked. They were 'old school' type of people, not so bothered about how much they sold the house for but that it should go to a custodian who would love and care for their family home, as they did.

My sister is a very busy lady but occasionally she will walk round with her dog, have a hasty cup of coffee and tell me what I should be doing with my life. She says I need to go back again, that I cannot leave it like this. It will never be over for me.

I asked her if she ever resented being robbed of her childhood and having to look after me and my brother. I'm sure she could get a few weeks off work and some counselling for 'post-traumatic stress.' She said it was her pleasure. The parents have come and gone but we three are as the sides of a triangle.

All the cousins have got together and created a fund in Iyah's name at Jaffna College. The money will be used to sponsor two children's education annually. We have not stipulated the religion, sex, caste or nationality of the children, that is how Iyah would have wanted it. June is prize giving time and she says I, a Sanders girl, should go and give the prize in his name. I'll think about that another day.

Time passes quickly when you are busy. It almost feels as if the first half of my life had little connection with the second half. I wonder what the last bit will bring. The great thing about getting older is that you care less, it is liberating. I reflect on how fortunate I have been and how much I have had, whatever happens next, no one can take that away.

I have spent too many years looking forward and the same again looking backward. So, now, I make myself a promise, that today is the best day of my life.

I am starting to ramble, so this is a good time to stop but not without saying to little brother, I broke your robot on Christmas Day and told all your admirers that I was your girlfriend. Much of what I have written, you wrote or said first, and I will end with a final act of plagiarism by finishing with your favourite song.

*Drinking in the morning sun*
*Blinking in the morning sun*
*Shaking off the heavy one*
*Heavy like a loaded gun*

*What made me behave that way?*
*Using words I never say*

193

*I can only think it must be love*
*Oh, anyway, it's looking like a beautiful day*

*Someone tell me how I feel*
*It's silly wrong but vivid right*
*Oh, kiss me like the final meal*
*Yeah, kiss me like we die tonight*

*Cause holy cow, I love your eyes*
*And only now I see the light*
*Yeah, lying with me half awake*
*Oh, anyway, it's looking like a beautiful day*

*When my face is chamois-creased*
*If you think I'll wink, I did*
*Laugh politely at repeats*
*Yeah, kiss me when my lips are thin*

*Cause holy cow, I love your eyes*
*And only now I see you like*
*Yeah, lying with me half awake*
*Stumbling over what to say*
*Well, anyway, it's looking like a beautiful day*

*Throw those curtains wide!*
*One day like this a year'd you see me right*
*Throw those curtains wide!*
*One day like this a year we'll sing it right.*

Elbow

# GLOSSARY

| | |
|---|---|
| Acca | Sister |
| Aiyoo | 'Oh my goodness' |
| Almera | Wooden wardrobe |
| Ammah | Mother |
| Ammammah | Mother's mother |
| Annan | Brother |
| Anthurium | 'Flamingo flower' vibrant, different colours |
| Appah | Father |
| Appammah | Father's mother |
| Appu | Mother's father |
| Athan | Brother-in-law |
| Bhaila | Portuguese/Sri Lankan pop music |
| Bharathanatyam | Ancient Asian dance |
| Bulto | Burnt, toffee-like sweet |
| Carroum | A bit like finger billiards played with discs |
| Chandia | Feisty small child |
| Chi chi chi | Oh dear, oh dear, oh dear |

| | |
|---|---|
| Chinacca | Little sister |
| Chithappah | Father's little brother |
| Chutta | Little sweet |
| Dagobas | White, dome-like Buddhist temples |
| Dobbie | Washer man |
| Eelam | Independent Tamil kingdom |
| Idli | Rice cakes |
| Ivan | This chap |
| Iyah | Master |
| Kaddai | Shop |
| Karrupu | Dark complexion |
| Kunchu | Darling |
| Hoppers | Round pancakes made from rice flour with coconut milk in the middle |
| Lattu | Sweet made from semolina raisins and cashew nut |
| Lump rice | Packet containing sambar rice, meat, cutlets, boiled egg and vegetables in coconut milk |
| Mallum | Leek and coconut curry |
| Mametty | Large knife |
| Marma | Uncle |
| Marmie | Aunt |
| Namadayal | Yokel/fool |
| Palmyra tree | Abundant in the north tall thin palm tree |
| Parrupu | Lentil curry |
| Payasam | Pudding from semolina and jaggery |
| Periappah | Father's big brother |
| Pillai | Child |
| Pittu | Logs of rice flour in coconut |
| Pottu | Decorative dot on forehead worn by married Hindu women |
| Sambar rice | Pearl like type of rice |
| Seeni Sambol | Onion and fish chutney |
| Serendib | Arabic/Persian name for Sri Lanka |
| String hoppers | Starch-like knotted spaghetti |
| Taprobane | Greek name for Sri Lanka |

| | |
|---|---|
| Thai/Thei | Dance moves |
| Thali | Gold necklace worn instead of ring by married women. Also can be a silver plate used in ceremonies and for food |
| Thoddu | Sweets snack, crispy made to look like earrings |
| Thosai | Savoury pancake made from pulses |
| Thumbu muttas | Candy floss |
| Ur | Homeland |
| Vaddai | Savoury doughnut made from lentil flour |
| Vathura | Water in Sinhala |
| Vatillupum | Pudding with rice flakes and jiggery |
| Vellai | Pale complexion |
| Vimto | Fizzy drink |
| Yaldevi | The night train |

# ABOUT THE AUTHOR

Surochini Sandero was born in 1965 in Jaffna, Ceylon.

She lives in Edinburgh, is married with two children and works as a Community Geriatrician.